Out Here

Out Here
Local and International Perspectives in Queer Studies

Edited by

Dominika Ferens, Tomasz Basiuk and Tomasz Sikora

Cambridge Scholars Publishing

Out Here: Local and International Perspectives in Queer Studies,
Edited by Dominika Ferens, Tomasz Basiuk and Tomasz Sikora

This book first published 2006. The present binding first published 2008.

Cambridge Scholars Publishing

12 Back Chapman Street, Newcastle upon Tyne, NE6 2XX, UK

British Library Cataloguing in Publication Data
A catalogue record for this book is available from the British Library

Copyright © 2008 by Dominika Ferens, Tomasz Basiuk and Tomasz Sikora and contributors

All rights for this book reserved. No part of this book may be reproduced, stored in a retrieval system, or transmitted, in any form or by any means, electronic, mechanical, photocopying, recording or otherwise, without the prior permission of the copyright owner.

ISBN (10): 1-84718-787-0, ISBN (13): 9781847187871

TABLE OF CONTENTS

Introduction
Tomasz Sikora, Tomasz Basiuk, Dominika Ferens 1

Normally
Tadeusz Rachwał 8

Traveling Images: Desire as Movement. Desire as Method?
Antke Engel 13

Handling the Touchy Subject: Dealing with the Author's Alleged or Actual Homosexuality in Polish Studies in the History of English Literature
Krzysztof Fordoński 25

Tamil and Queer: Political and Sexual Marginalization in Shyam Selvadurai's *Funny Boy*
Anna Branach-Kallas 39

"Into Another Woman:" Writing the Homoerotic in Vernon Lee's *Lady Tal*
Ewa Macura 49

Crisis House: Metaphors of Queer Depression
Zuzanna Szatanik 56

Just a stage? Biphobia in theory and practice
Anna Borgos 68

The Citadel Park. A Specific Node in a Network for (Queer) Desire
Els De Vos 79

Just Popping? Anti-homophobic Elements in Spanish and Catalan Contemporary Popular Music
Alfons Gregori i Gomis 97

All the Men Are White, Looks Like the Women Are Too, But Some of Us Know Better
Chris Bell 110

Violence against Homosexual Women: Stories from Everyday Life
Irina Kupriyanova 120

Sex Slavery and Queer Resistance in Eastern Europe
Tomek Kitliński, Joe Lockard 127

Gossip Through a Cracked Door: Revisiting Girls' Boarding School Culture
Dominika Ferens 144

Kiss Whiter than Snow
Ruth DyckFehderau 154

Contributors 164

INTRODUCTION

TOMASZ SIKORA, TOMASZ BASIUK, DOMINIKA FERENS

The present volume is a sequel to *A Queer Mixture / Odmiany odmieńca* (2002), which documented the first two queer studies conferences in Poland in 2000 and 2001. Three subsequent annual conferences took place in Warsaw (2002), Bielsko-Biała (2003) and Wrocław (2004), every one of them bringing together close to a hundred scholars and queer activists from Europe and North America. We are pleased to see these events become something of an institutionalized presence in a predominantly conservative Polish cultural and academic landscape, one in which LGBTQ undertakings are always exposed to political, economic and legal threats. For it is impossible to ignore that each of our last three conferences coincided with a crisis around queer people's rights.

In December 2002, in Warsaw, we devoted one panel to a discussion of a series of homophobic articles and antihomophobic responses published by the biggest Polish daily, the liberal *Gazeta Wyborcza* edited by Adam Michnik. In May 2003 we met in Bielsko-Biała on the night of Poland's EU accession referendum; we had cast our votes before coming to the conference and were all glued to TV screens that night at the hotel, waiting for the preliminary results to come in. The vote passed by a substantial majority.

Earlier that year, the artist Karolina Breguła collaborated with an organization called Campaign Against Homophobia in photographing 15 lesbian couples and 15 gay male couples. Each couple is shown standing in a city street, holding hands. A red stamp in the corner reads: "Let them see us." These 30 photographs were exhibited in galleries across Poland. Two images: one of a lesbian couple and one of a gay male couple, were selected for display on billboards in major cities. In many locations, homophobes managed to prevent the posters from being mounted by decrying them as "visual aggression," and virtually everywhere the posters were torn down or smudged with paint in a matter of days. But there was a heated media debate about whether these images should be allowed to be displayed, and some of the photographed subjects were interviewed about the personal consequences of their courageous exposure. In effect, even though the campaign was cut short, its ripple effect gave a new level of visibility to the Polish lesbian and gay male community.

The May 2004 conference was in Wroclaw, only days after Poland joined the European Union. A week after the accession Cracow had its first gay parade ever. It was interrupted by the All-Polish Youth (MW: Młodzież Wszechpolska), a nationalist militia of the League of Polish Families (LPR: Liga Polskich Rodzin), an extreme right-wing party with deputies in the Polish and the European parliaments. In the 1930s, the anti-Semitic All-Polish Youth was outlawed. Today it has been resurrected, in part to target queers, and has even brought eleven members into the Polish parliament under LPR auspices in the 2005 election. At the time of the violent outbreak in Cracow, a conference on homosexuality at the sociology department of Poland's oldest university, the Jagiellonian, was relegated from the main campus to a distant location on the outskirts of Cracow. That same month, May 2004, the fifth annual Warsaw Equality Parade, which has always had a primarily gay presence, was to take place. We were at the Wrocław conference when we heard that the parade had been banned by the politically ambitious right-wing mayor of Warsaw, recently elected president of Poland. During the same conference, a late-night discussion on queer strategizing taking place in a local bar was disrupted by two homophobic thugs who identified themselves a members of NOP, a right-wing political organization. This unfortunate, if minor, incident seemed merely symptomatic of the deteriorating conditions for a rational discussion on LGBTQ rights in the country, but it has confronted us directly with the harsh reality outside the ivory tower of academia, and sometimes within. Like many other organizations and individuals, we sent the Warsaw mayor a letter of protest, which had no effect. This parade was banned three times because the regional governor twice reversed the mayor's homophobic decision. In the end, a political rally took place in front of the mayor's office on the scheduled day.

Tomek Kitliński and Paweł Leszkowicz have commented on the violent assaults on the Cracow gay march in May 2004 and the subsequent ban of the Warsaw Equality Parade that same month by calling homophobia in Poland "one symptom of a larger social crisis of failed justice" (19). Since 1989, when a new democratic regime changed the context for gay activism, a double logic of increased openness toward and a backlash against queers has been in place. Our series of conferences has been paralleled by an increased gay activism and visibility, as well as by a moral panic around homosexuality, sexual abuse, paedophilia, and HIV. These phenomena are frequently superimposed in public discourse, and occasionally serve as a smokescreen obscuring even more shameful topics, like anti-Semitism. Thus, a Catholic archbishop was forced into retirement for his homosexuality rather than for his actual transgression of molesting clerics who answered to him. Another distinguished clergyman, whose anti-Semitic statements and flamboyant lifestyle were known but drew only mild criticism, lost his parish when he was accused of seducing an altar boy. A famous choir conductor, charged with sexually molesting boy singers, had his seropositive status exposed by the mainstream liberal daily *Gazeta Wyborcza*, which acted illegally but, allegedly, in the public's interest. And a theatre director writing regularly for the same daily, in which he courageously came out as a gay man, was soon after attacked by his own paper for volunteering to donate blood. He had been entrapped by his colleagues from the newspaper who first invited him to participate in a blood drive and then turned against him in editorials in which they explained that a gay man's blood is a public health risk. As we were writing the present introduction, two things have happened simultaneously: another collection of essays, *Homofobia po polsku,* the first-ever book on homophobia in Poland, published in October 2004, sold out within just a few weeks, and the "Equality March" in Poznań was attacked and disrupted by the All-Polish Youth militia on November 20, 2004. In the spring of 2005, as a parallel Polish volume was going to press, the Warsaw parade was banned for the second year running. Activists took to the streets anyway, joined by many supporters, some prominent Polish and German politicians among them.

There is more than one way to tell the story of this volume, just as our activist and intellectual strategies are diverse, and as we are learning more than one thing from one another. But perhaps one general point can be made, that the context in which we have to function makes our work (and the present book in particular) politically incorrect in our own country. Ironically, our work is often dismissed as tainted with "political correctness." Some of us have never intended to be politically correct or politically incorrect, to cast ourselves in the terms of this particular binary, but at the moment it feels like the matter is out of our hands.

The concept of "political correctness," which constitutes one of the barriers for—or parameters of—queer desire, has tremendous currency in Poland's intellectual and political debate. Given the recent conservative backlash in this country, Kinga Dunin, one of Poland's most outspoken feminists, wrote in a December 2003 editorial: "I choose what ill-meaning people would surely call political correctness. . . . I wish for political correctness" (46). Rather than knowingly choose the misnomer "political correctness" we may want to examine it critically. During the two decades since it was coined, the term has been used to deter women, non-whites, queer people, and others from reaching for privileges traditionally reserved for white heterosexual men. The intellectual work of those "others," perceived as usurpers of public space, has routinely been devalued as "politically correct."

The cultural conservatives who coined the American term "political correctness" brought to life a phantom power that supposedly stands behind the usurpers. "Political correctness" is a smokescreen obscuring the fact that the cultural conservatives themselves constitute the dominant majority and dictate the terms on which queers enter the public sphere. In Poland, those who use the term insist that they are being gagged by a powerful pressure group. For instance, in an article titled "The Gay Men's Bishop" published in the weekly *Polityka* Adam Szostkiewicz used the consecration of the Episcopalian Bishop Gene Robinson in New Hampshire as a pretext to lash out against "the practitioners" of political correctness, "a false doctrine that silences "the voices of Christians who want to speak about poverty and moderation" (57). Located somewhere in what Szostkiewicz calls the "American-European West" there is a phantom power that has turned Poland's moral order upside down. "The issue of homosexuals' rights has become. . . a litmus test of the degree of desirable consciousness change. According to the adherents of [political correctness], whoever is in favor of full legal equality understands what the modern liberal society is all about. Whoever opposes such equality deviates from the pluralistic norm. Whoever is uncertain is an intellectual sloth who hasn't done his homework" (57).

The common rhetorical strategy of invoking a phantom enables Szostkiewicz and other cultural conservatives to deflect attention from the fact that it is both "politically correct" and politically advantageous in Poland today to deny queer people the right of public assembly and free speech, to erase queer histories and to deny the existence of queer cultures. No phantom stopped the daily *Gazeta Wyborcza* from giving prominence to pundits defending homophobia as reasonable. No phantom managed to dissuade the Chancellor of the Jagiellonian University from removing an LGBTQ studies conference out of sight, to a campus on the outskirts of Cracow. No phantom prevented the All-Polish Youth from pelting LGBTQ rights demonstrators with stones in the streets of Cracow, and then in Poznań. No phantom stopped the Mayor of Warsaw from banning the 2004 and the 2005 Equality Parades.

This neo-conservative rhetoric—dressed in very "progressive" terms—has also found its way into the Polish academic environment. Polish academia did not have the time to critically investigate the stakes of "political (in)correctness" when a symptomatic conference, ominously entitled "Mouth Wide Shut," was announced, boldly declaring political correctness to be "democracy's policeman" in a call for papers that offered foregone conclusions rather than an invitation to critical analyses and open-minded debates: "The many tongues of multicultural discourse speak all the more loudly since the potential opponents, having been successfully bound and gagged, dare not express any contradictory opinion." Ironically enough, the "Call for Papers"—itself totally unrealistic about the political balance of power in Poland and elsewhere—ends with the invocation to "take up the challenge before the academe itself is declared a reservation [asylum] for the realistically challenged." The sarcasm directed at the "politically correct" revision of linguistic conventions itself defers to a fantasmatic Realpolitik. This deferral is motivated by the hope—which we think is false—that academics can make themselves publicly relevant by adopting widespread stereotypes.

The eminent Polish law historian Jan Baszkiewicz was one of the few to see through the phantom of "political correctness"—albeit in a context unrelated to non-normative sexuality. During a recent ceremony at which he received an honorary doctorate from Wrocław University, Baszkiewicz told an anecdote set in the 1960s in which he described as a bold act of "political *incorrectness*" a Chancellor's defiance of the socialist party's orders to suppress a symbol of the university's German past. He thus implied that being "politically correct" means aligning oneself with whoever happens to represent the hegemonic order.

Clearly, given the habitual (mindless or malign) misuse of the term "political correctness" we might do better to drop it altogether. And if we cannot get rid of this slippery term we should aim to reverse its current usage, and seek to clarify its meaning as "hegemonic correctness." It may be tempting to pretend, along with the homophobic majority, that there is a phantom power watching over the Polish queer community and enabling Poles to resist racism, sexism, homophobia and extreme nationalism. But perhaps instead of endorsing phantoms we should draw strength from being "politically incorrect," and focus on preventing the gay-rights debate from being dismissed with the facile charge of its "correctness."

A remarkable difference between *Out Here* and its predecessor is that many more Polish and other East-European authors in the present volume have undertaken direct political and cultural reflection on the historical contingencies of the local context. Unlike the previous bilingual volume, this one contains only those papers which were originally presented in English; a parallel volume of papers in Polish will be published by the Cracow Universitas publishing house. Among the essays in English, Tomek Kitliński and Joe Lockard offer a polemical diagnosis of homophobia and misogyny embodied in various Polish state and cultural institutions, Irina Kupriyanova describes the difficulties in implementing proper standards for counseling lesbian women in Russia, and Anna Borgos writes about bisexuality and biphobia from a Hungarian perspective. Alfons Gregori i Gomis undertakes a queer-political critique of Spanish and Catalan pop, and Els De Vos explains the spatial and cultural complexities of cruising ina Belgian park. Krzysztof Fordoński is interested in how the question of authors' well-documented or alleged homosexuality is (or—

more often—is not) addressed in Polish handbooks and anthologies of English literature. Antke Engel starts by outlining the concepts of desire in Foucault and in Deleuze/Guattari, and argues that desire can be politically effective only if we attend to the ways in which singularities are transformed into specific categories. Tadeusz Rachwał's "Normally," the keynote address of our Bielsko-Biała conference in May 2003, is also a philosophical argument which draws on Kierkegaard, Deleuze and Guattari, Braidotti, and Irigaray for the possibility of redrafting the present regimes of queer intelligibility. Tadeusz Rachwał's contribution, Anna Branach-Kallas's reading of Shaym Selvaduri's *Funny Boy*, Ewa Macura's reading of Vernon Lee's *Lady Tal*, Zuzanna Szatanik's paper on Chandra Mayor's poetry, and Krzysztof Fordoński's survey of Polish hanbooks of English literature remind us that English and American studies departments in Poland were not only among the first places where interest in queer subjects was allowed to flourish, but that they remain interested and supportive. The English-language section also includes two short stories by Ruth DyckFehderau, one of a number of queer scholars who have recently stayed in Poland as visiting professors. Chris Bell is another such scholar, and his contribution to this volume, which tackles the psycho-social knot of sexuality and race/ethnicity, is one that inspired in us a sense of future direction.

Looking through the prism of sexuality and gender, the authors of *Out Here* offer analyses remarkably in sync with the present historical moment. For we are at a cross-roads, requiring that we look in more than one direction. Intersections of gender, sexuality, class, and ethnicity, are familiar to many in academia but not always a staple in intellectual debates and teaching. While the concurrence of gender and queer issues in Poland seems well established, though not exactly in the center of the political arena—even as it seems, remarkably, to be the country's longest-standing coalition since 1989—this coalition is marginalized not only by the hegemony of cultural conservatives, but also by its own difficulty in addressing issues of economic inequality and other forms of discrimination. There is no adequate cultural criticism of the remnants of class-based distinctions in our post-Communist society, or of the new forms of such distinctions. Also the nationalistic projection of Poland as an ethnically homogeneous country that has no real need to address questions of ethnicity is perniciously widespread. It seems symptomatic to us that issues of class and race/ethnicity are more readily raised by non-Poles contributing to this volume.

We recognize these limitations, as we recognize that the breakthrough billboard campaign of 2003, mentioned above, was limited by the somewhat gentrified, vanilla look of almost all photographed couples, the young age of all but one, and the notable absence of a single photograph taken in the countryside (in a country where a full quarter of the population lives in rural areas). One should note, however, that the photographs are an archival record of the state of

LGBTQ activism in Poland today, and that the lives of some individuals who were photographed as part of the campaign have changed for it. While analogous claims should not be made for the present volume, some of the essays ring with a sense of urgency, reflecting the tone of current debates about Poland's LGBTQ activism. The analyses contained herein are elements in the landscape of such debates, in Poland and elsewhere.

The 2004 Wrocław conference was marked by fault lines in our discussions of sexuality in relation to gender, class, ethnicity, and other categories which define positionality. As at other conferences, we ended with an open forum whose goal was to propose a topic for the next event. In this discussion, positionality was again pointed out by many as a crucial question for further debate, and it became the focus of our next annual meeting, in September 2005.

We would like to acknowledge our gratitude to Professor Paweł Dybel of the Polish Academy of Sciences and of Warsaw University for his critical comments and invaluable suggestions.

Works Cited

Dunin, Kinga. "Życzę sobie." *Wysokie Obcasy* [supplement to *Gazeta Wyborcza*] 27 Dec. 2003: 46.
Kitliński, Tomek, and Paweł Leszkowicz. "Queer Studies in Eastern Europe." *CLAGSnews* [newsletter of the Center for Lesbian and Gay Studies, City University of New York] Summer 2004: 19.
Szostkiewicz, Adam. "Biskup gejów." *Polityka* 22 Nov. 2003: 56-57.
Zbigniew Sypniewski and Błażej Warkocki, eds. *Homofobia po polsku*. Warszawa: sic!, 2004.

NORMALLY

Tadeusz Rachwał

> My suspicion is that the universe is not only queerer than we suppose, but queerer than we can suppose.
>
> Physiologist and Geneticist J.B.S. Haldane, *Possible Worlds*, 1927 (qtd. in Goddwin)

"Normally" is an adverb which is normally used with reference to regular, repetitive occurrences of things and events in normal and ordinary conditions. The very fact of the word's use in natural languages testifies to an existence of "sets of facts or fixed limits which establish or limit how something can or must happen or be done" (*Freesearch Dictionary*)—that is to say, to the existence of parameters which normalize our acts and actions and thus enable a harmoniously repetitive existence. Though, as Kierkegaard claimed, "in reality as such, there is no repetition" (Kierkegaard 275), the parametrisation of the social space translates repetition into the normal, a normally frequented furrow which determines what "must happen or be done."

In Kierkegaard repetition occurs only when "ideality and reality touch each other" (Kierkegaard 275), ideality being the sphere of sameness which, like reality as such, also excludes repetition. Though Kierkegaard does not explicitly gender either ideality or reality, he does claim that creative, philosophical natures should be somehow feminine, so as to be capable of being inseminated by the unchangeable masculine ideal. What is thus produced in the mutual touching of the ideal and the real is the "normally" of repetition, the regulative parameter which is a trace, or a seed, of the ideal within the creatively effeminate masculine philosopher. Repetition proves the existence of the ideal sameness through a touching contact with men rather than women, the latter slipping away from the parametrization and remaining within the real which, without the ideal, constitutes an undifferentiated difference without any stable criteria of a repeatable identity:

... for I have rarely seen a girl whose life could be comprehended in a category. She usually lacks the consistency required for admiring or scorning a person. Before a woman deceives another, she first deceives herself, and therefore there is no criterion at all. (Kierkegaard 218)

Capability to repeat constitutes the possibility of identification, of being identified, the identifiable always holding a privileged position over the deceitful feminine which, as lacking criteria, demands a parametrization so as to become mappable upon some public space. In Kierkegaard this "mappability" is determined by the openness to the masculine insemination by ideas available only to creative and philosophically minded feminized creatures who desire the touch of ideas so as to be able "to be comprehended in a category." The touch of the clearly masculine ideal in fact masculinizes the feminine philosophers and sublimates them above the reality, normalizes them as bearers of the ideal, of the unchangeable norm. What thus becomes desired is the touching union with the ideal which represses the real, that which cannot be repeated, which does not happen normally.

Deleuze and Guattari find in this repression a defensive gesture of the society for which an un-parametrized desire is threatening:

If desire is repressed, it is because every position of desire. . . is capable of calling into question the established order of society. . . it is revolutionary in its essence. . . . It is therefore of vital importance for a society to repress desire, and even to find something more efficient than repression, so that repression, hierarchy, exploitation, and servitude are themselves desired. (Deleuze 116)

The repressed desire puts on a mask of reproductive activities whose function is, as Foucault claims in *The History of Sexuality*, to discourage useless waste of energy which would obstruct capitalism. Translated into ethical terms, unreproductive activities become immoral and perverse, naturally unnatural things which you, normally, do not do. Yet, as Shannon Roberts notices writing on Bataille, "Even in a monologue that condemns sexual immorality, the silent figure which it addresses stands outside of the norm, its existence being justified and noticed by the sole fact that its alterity is emphasized" (Roberts). The alterity enters the discourse through repression and thus, paradoxically, also enters the repeatable pattern of the parametrization of desire with all its categorizations, criteria, and hierarchies. More importantly, it thus also becomes a part of the repressive normalcy.

An interesting attempt at parametrising desire comes from Alan Sinfield, who notices "confusion in many current ideas of gayness" and attempts at clarifying that confusion making use of Freud's distinction between *desire-for* and *desire-to-be* (Sinfield 120). Beginning with the heterosexual model in which

| A man has: | desire-to-be M | desire-for F |
| A woman has: | desire-to-be F | desire-for M |

and going through various possible combinations of it he ends with the possibility in which

| man has: | desire-to-be not-M | desire-for God |

He adds: "For the point of a taxonomy, I have said, is not to confine identity or desire but, rather, to offer a framework within which the specificity and multiplicity of the potential combinations and interactions may coherently emerge" (Sinfield 137).

This coherence of emergence of identity and desire, regardless of its more or less endless paradigmatic potential, introduces the regulatory repetition to the functioning of desire thus making it parametrical. As taxonomically repeatable, Sinfield's parameters of desire make desire a matter of a certain survival enabled by the coherent pattern of the possible fulfillments of desire. What this survival promotes is the permanence of the forms of desire which Zygmunt Bauman opposes to happiness as life strategy. "Survival," he writes, "is about sticking to the norm; happiness is an inherently anti-normative power. Survival dreams of ultimate rest and finds its fulfillment in standing still. But the moment of rest is the agony of happiness" (87).[1]

Perhaps it is the very idea of fulfillment of desire, of accomplishment, which renders desire as always already parametrized, this or that oriented. With the orientation at stake, desire becomes a way to repeat, a normally followed path, a matter of survival which leaves happiness behind, in the realm of Kierkegaard's reality, for example. For what comes along with survival and repetition is value, the measurable and identifiable measure of things which also harbours appropriation, the ownership of oneself and of the satisfaction of their desire which is rooted, as we have seen, also in Kierkegaard's homosocial, and in fact Platonic, vision of repetition.

Perhaps Rosi Braidotti's economy which conceives of desire ontologically— not as mediation between a subject and a desired object, but as transcending the subject, as a "desire which functions as the threshold for a redefinition of a new common plane of experience" (Braidotti 203)—is a non-species of desire which the homosocial discourse of Kierkeaardian philosophy leaves unmentioned within the feminine real to which "normally" does not normally apply. A surfacing of this desire happens on the threshold of the real, slightly away from the technology of desire which parametrizes it into, let us repeat, "a set of facts or a fixed limit which establishes or limits how something can or must happen or be done." For what comes with repetition is also distance, the clarity of objective vision in which even things queer are, say, normally queer. A disturbance of this normality, a really common plane of experience, is thinkable only along with the possibility of there being a non-objective economy, an economy which, by way of overcoming distances, will blur the clear-cut division into the public and the private through a certain de-privatization, or perhaps deprivation, of the private whose hope Luce Irigaray envisages in the feminine:

> Ownership and property are doubtless quite foreign to the feminine. At least sexually. But not nearness. Nearness so pronounced that it makes all discrimination of identity, and thus all forms of property, impossible. Woman derives pleasure from what is so near that she cannot have it, nor have herself. She herself enters into a ceaseless exchange of herself with the other without any possibility of identifying either. This puts into question all prevailing economies. (Irigaray 31)

How? Normally?

Notes

1. I have found an interesting "survival kit" of sorts which also in a way epitomizes the Kierkegaardian parametrization of desire in a letter published on the *Chrsitian Woman Today* webpage: "Children need love, affection and guidance and parameters. Women respond to love and gentleness, but we too, need parameters. Many times the satisfaction of momentary pleasures can be tempting, but the results can be devastating. God has set up boundaries in His word because He loves us. They are there to keep us safe. Practicing self-control means saying "No" to the things that God says "No" to. God's rules are for our benefit. We can follow them fearlessly."

Works Cited

Bauman, Zygmunt. "Excess: An Obituary." *Parallax* 7. 1 (2001): 85-91.
Braidotti, Rosi. Nomadic Subjects. Embodiment and Sexual Diffrence in Contemporary Feminist Theor. New York: Columbia University Press, 1994.
Chrsitian Woman Today <http://archive.christianwomentoday.com/devotions/love.html>.
Deleuze, Gilles and Félix Guattari. *Anti-Oedipus: Capitalism and Schizophrenia*. Minneapolis: University of Minnesota Press, 1972.
Freesearch Dictionary <http://www.freesearch.co.uk/dictionary/parameters> (from *Cambridge Advanced Learner's Dictionary*. Cambridge: Cambridge University Press, 2003).

Goodwin, Joseph P. "Let's Get Physical: A Quantum Look at the Queer Space-Time Continuum." *New Directions in Folklore* 4.1 (2000) <http://www.temple.edu/isllc/newfolk/physical.html>.

Irigaray, Luce. *This Sex Which Is Not One.* Trans. Catherine Porter and Carolyn Burke. Ithaca: Cornell University Press, 1985.

Kierkegaard, Søren. *Repetition.* Trans. Howard V. Hong and Edna H. Hong. Princeton: Princeton University Press, 1983.

Roberts, Shannon. "Foucault, Deleuze and Guattari on the Interruptive Repression of Desire by Forcing it into Discourse." <http://www.angelfire.com/art/serelou/persoframes/thesis/SUBLIMREPRES.HTML>.

Sinfield, Alan. "Lesbian and Gay Taxonomies." *Critical Inquiry* 29.1 (2002): 120-138.

TRAVELING IMAGES: DESIRE AS MOVEMENT. DESIRE AS METHOD?

ANTKE ENGEL

By now, it is not only liberal but also conservative voices who accept homosexuality as a sexual identity and a certain life-style—as long as it remains private and "they" do not claim civil rights or political participation. In quite a few countries homosexuals receive official state recognition of their right to private freedom, but this does not mean that they enjoy full and equal citizenship. The inclusion is bound to a distinction between the public and the private. It relegates homosexuality to the private sphere, which is understood in terms of rights as the free choice of consenting adults, and in terms of capital as commodified desires and commercialized spaces that pay into? capitalist economy. The "law" of these private spheres says: Do not question the superiority of heterosexuality and its privileges like marriage and parenting rights, tax benefits and legal heritage. In the discourse of privatization, a gesture of liberal tolerance is easily combined with homophobic stereotyping, discrimination, and exclusion.

Desire: The Challenge to the Public/Private-Distinction

Queer Theory deploys "desire" as an important category of political analysis. I would like to ask if there is a concept of desire that challenges the opposition of the public and the private—a concept that values the diversity and singularity of desires, while also looking at desire as a normative category organizing subjectivities and the social. In fact, I am not so much interested in desire as a category of subjectivity, of sexual practices or intimate relations. Rather, I try to understand how desire is productive in the social and of the social—including macro-political processes and institutions. How far is desire at work where we don't expect it, in the state, in capitalism, in global relations? Does heterosexual desire rule here?

To consider these questions I turn to Elspeth Probyn, who in her book *Outside Belongings* (1996) deploys desire in a way that does not reassert normative heterosexuality or rigid gender binaries. Probyn avoids reducing desire to a moment of identity or to relationships organized by a subject/object dynamic, and she looks for a concept of desire which challenges the psychoanalytic perspectives of lack and interiority. In this vein she refers to Gilles Deleuze and Felíx Guattari in order to understand desire as movement and productivity. Personal as well as broader cultural images are seen as modes of "transportation" which link individual and social, virtual, material, mental, and psychic "bodies." Movements of desire, traveling in images, effect a complex, dynamic and interrelational "surface." Desire becomes a way to question the concept of identity and binary distinctions, including the distinction of public and private.

Starting from here I will explain how Probyn's concept links power and desire and can be used to analyze governance and state policies. Finally, I will discuss Probyn's suggestion that we understand desire as a method. Is she referring to methods in social sciences or cultural or political practices? Is "desire" a convincing ground for queer social analysis? What does it mean if we want to understand, or to challenge, or to change social regulations of gender and sexuality or the gendering and sexualization of social power relations? Does she use "method" in the sense of "strategy"?

Desire as Movement

Outside Belongings is the programmatic title of Probyn's book. But just how might such a program propose an alternative to an identity-based model of subjectivity and social relations? In Probyn, the term "belonging" evokes two different associations: "belongings"—this means goods, memories, the history one carries (while moving or staying on) as well as "longing"—the yearning for something or someone or somewhere—perhaps even the longing to belong. While Probyn eschews an identity model that captures subjectivity within the limits of normative categories and a demand for authenticity, she still takes the wish to belong seriously. For her, this is a wish that people cultivate while knowing that it is challenged by various forces and can hardly ever be fulfilled:

> Simply put, I want to figure the desire that individuals have to belong, a tenacious and fragile desire that is, I think, increasingly performed in the knowledge of the impossibility of ever really and truly belonging, along with the fear that the stability of belonging and the sanctity of belongings are forever past. (Probyn 8)

So much for "belonging." And how are we to understand "outside"? "Outside" is not defined in relation to an inside or interiority, but actually challenges the opposition of in and out. It is rather to be understood as "surface," which has no organizing center, but flees in all directions, as Deleuze/Guattari would put it.

Thinking on the surface—or surfacing, as Probyn proposes in order to avoid an objectivation of the surface—offers an alternative to modes of thinking which dig for an inner truth, a cause, a ground in the depths of an unknowable history:

> One of the central arguments of this book is that the outside is a more adequate figure for thinking about social relations and the social than either an interior/exterior or a center/marginal model. The notion of the outside supposes that we think in terms of "relations of proximity," or the surface, "a network in which each point is distinct. . . and has a position in relation to every other point in the space that simultaneously holds and separates them all (Foucault 1987: 12)." (Probyn 11)

Within this model of thinking on the surface (rather than searching for reasons or causes or identities) desire becomes a force of movement, a principle that translates across things, words, bodies, and meanings, creating connections, tracing lines of flight and lines of belonging (45).

Traveling Images

While in psychoanalysis it is a single sign, the phallus, that signifies desire, for Probyn it is complex images that travel within and between social, cultural, and material worlds that produce connections and meanings. Those images are always singular. They have neither an essence nor a fixed reference, but they trace lines of flight and they are productive. These lines of flight are not virtual, but show up as material-semiotic effects on social surfaces: Images relate bodies and incite desire; they alter "categorized notions of being" and open up new notions of becoming and belonging:

> The image, thus freed from its post within a structure of law, lack, and signification, can begin to move all over the place. It then causes different ripples and affects, effects of desire and desirous affects. Turning away from the game of matching signifiers and signifieds, we can begin to focus on the movement of images as effecting and affecting movement. (59)

Desire is the force that incites and fuels this movement, these transports. The complexity of an image illustrates that in a specific situation there is more than one power axis involved in desire's social productivity. Power, in this case, is the condition and effect of these movements of transportation inspired by desire: "this is to render desire entirely social, as lubricating lines of governance and power, and those of subjectivation" (45).

Assemblages of Desire and Power: Deleuze vs. Foucault

Probyn's concept does not know a private realm that is not always already connected to public discourses, practices, and institutions. Even the most closeted subjectivities and desires cannot be understood apart from those socio-cultural forces that demand their hiding and limit their access to or visibility on social surfaces. But while Probyn understands desire as entirely social and rejects any kind of naturalized or essentialized view, she is still hesitant to adopt Michel Foucault's view of desire as solely a product of power relations. According to Foucault, desires are constituted within systems of power/knowledge which deploy desire as the inner truth of an individual and as constitutive of subjectivities, social relations, knowledges, technologies of the self, and forms of governance. Probyn would agree to this, but still cede importance to Deleuze'/Guattari's arguement that desire cannot be reduced to a product and a productive means of power relations, but should be seen as a force in its own right.

According to Deleuze/Guattari, desire is a force that connects and disconnects objects and enunciations, a force that produces "lines of flight" and "assemblages" of "things," and "enunciations," and "affections." To describe an assemblage one has to ask how enunciations and things connect—this is one axis of analysis. Another line of inquiry concerns the mode of movement taking place: Is it a "deterritorialization" that breaks up well established connections, or is it a "re-territorialization," that hegemonizes a formerly provocative or subversive assemblage? Interestingly, from Deleuze's perspective, power is primarily at work in reterritorializations and not so much in deterritorializations:

> Systems of power would emerge everywhere that reterritorializations are operating. . . . Systems of power would thus be a component of assemblages. But assemblages would also comprise points of deterritorialization. In short, systems of power would neither motivate, nor constitute, but rather desiring-assemblages would swarm among the formations of power according to their dimensions. (Deleuze 4)

Foucault, on the contrary, would argue that any form of deterritorialization is no less involved in and conditioned by power relations than any reterritorializations. But, in fact, the advantage of Deleuze/Guattari's model is that it differentiates power and resistance, which is certainly a useful step for political analysis. Probyn, who combines Foucault and Deleuze/Guattari, agrees with Foucault that there is no social apart from power relations, but suggests that we understand power as one force next to other forces, e.g. desire, which interconnectedly constitute social relations. She would probably agree with Deleuze, who writes: "Of course, a desiring-assemblage will include power systems..., but they would have to be situated in relation to different components of the assemblage" (4).

Thus what has by now become clear is that Probyn's *Outside Belongings* challenges the "double privatization" of desire: desire to be kept in private space, and desire seen as a person's innermost identity. Rather, we can explore its productivity in and of social relations, including relations of power and resistance. Countering the critique that the metaphor of the surface enforces a certain superficiality, Probyn argues that surfaces are not flat and can very well capture hierarchical, uneven relations, dominating or subordinated positions (Probyn 18, 34). Still the question remains whether desire and movement are a value in and of themselves, or whether one must also ask what kind of desire is in question here and where it is moving to?

In *Profit and Pleasures: Sexual Identities in Late Capitalism,* Rosemary Hennessy is most skeptical about celebrations of the mobility of desire, which are, from her point of view, caught up in a capitalist logic of consumer society. Desire, within her materialist-feminist frame, primarily stimulates consumption and enforces reifications of social relations. For her it is "desirable" that we analyze the socio-historical forces that produce desire, that we ask, who profits, who extracts surplus value, who gets exploited while we are enjoying the pleasures of being a desiring subject. This project appears to provide a useful way of understanding how desire and power are co-implicated.

But Hennessy's argument implies an assimilation of consumers' desire and sexual desire, leaving no fissure, no gap between them. The "new consuming subject of desire" (Hennessy 110) in Late Capitalism translates its sexual desire into consumption, where practices of consumption function as a form of sexual stimulation and—unfulfillable, permanently deferred—satisfaction. While Hennessy is certainly right that today we can hardly imagine any desire independent from capitalism, it is neither convincing that there are no other forces at work in desire (forces which might contradict or subvert a capitalist logic) nor that consumption can be reduced to a logic of desire. The question remains: Can desire be reduced to being a product—be it a product of capitalist processes or of power/knowledge systems? What if this product conditions further productions? Do they necessarily replicate the logic of their becoming or can we expect forms of resistance?

Public Space, Social Relations, and the State's Desire

Liberal tolerance proudly offers a variety of private and commercialized leisure-time pleasures to deviant sexualities. If one wants to oppose this gesture of generosity, this means occupying public spaces and loudly/proudly articulating those various desires that won't stay in the closet any longer. But more important than demanding recognition and taking up public space would be the transformation of a hierarchized hegemonic public which, up to now, functions along the lines of discrimination, normalization, exclusion, and violence. Can we conceptualize desire as a productive force in power struggles over sexuality's social existence? Can we reject the smooth fit of desire into the public/private divide or even challenge this divide? Is it possible or promising to make use of the metaphor of space in order to "deterritorialize" desire?

Thinking about the public as "public space" refers to the very materiality of space without creating an opposition between the material and the discursive. Space, from a political as well as a geographical point of view, is seen as "semiotic materiality." Rural and urban areas, gay ghettos, lesbian lands, heterosexualized malls, and sanctified churches—all of these spaces simultaneously hold material, symbolic, and imaginary dimensions. Gill Valentine, a British geographer, supports the use of the concept of performativity in order to understand space not as a given, not as "stages or pre-existing places where [something, e.g. sexuality] is played out" (Valentine 154), but rather as an effect of performances and performative articulations (see also Gregson and Rose, cited by Valentine):

> The repetitive performances which produce everyday heterosexual space take the form of many acts: from heterosexual couples kissing and holding hands as they walk down the street, to advertisements and shop window displays that present images of contented "nuclear" families; and from heterosexualised conversations that permeate queues at bus stops and banks to the piped music articulating heterosexual desires that fill shops, bars and restaurants. . . . These acts are produced within regulatory regimes which serve to discipline and constrain the performances that are possible. . . . The power of heterosexuality therefore depends on being able to repeatedly define people and spaces in particular ways. However, because spaces do not pre-exist their performance but rather are iterative, there are always possibilities that disruptions and slippages may occur in their production, or that the disciplinary regimes that regulate them might fail, with the consequence that powerful discourses are not replicated but changed or done differently. (Valentine 155)

This sounds promising. But "the consequence" Valentine is suggesting is not quite necessary: Why, how, and under what circumstances do failures, or disruptions, or a sabotage of proper performances not only interrupt, but actually transform hegemonic discourses? When does a deterritorialization occur? Here it might be useful to turn again to Probyn, who at least offers a method for recognizing and mapping transformations. Her project of looking for images that travel and creating empirical interrelations on social surfaces enables her to indicate how slippages and disruptions deterritorialize a traditional territory, form new territories, and, maybe, effect reterritorialization. From her point of view, desire can be seen as the driving force of those productive movements, although this demands a break with traditional concepts—of desire as well as of politics:

> For desire is a profoundly upsetting force. It may totally rearrange what we think we want: desire skews plans, setting forth unthought-of possibilities. But as a term within traditional models. . . desire has tended to reassure the established order of things. It has either been totally missing or has served to operate as the ever unattainable referent: the lack that guarantees signification, a lack that is traditionally figured as women or other. (Probyn 43)

Here Probyn talks about psychoanalytic as well as poststructuralist models of communication. But what if we transfer her analysis to the field of the political and try to understand "desire as a profoundly upsetting force"? Traditional models of the political, the political as a mode of organizing society, deploy the opposition of public and private. They construct the public as an arena of the political, distinguished from a private that serves as its supposedly pre-political ground. Innumerable critiques have been articulated against this distinction; in fact, this critique might be no less constitutive of the political than the distinction itself. Feminist thinkers in particular have promoted the politicization of the so-called private. They have pointed out how "private tasks" like reproductive and emotional labor (including sex-work and love, including the reproduction of exploitable work-power as well as of individuals, their socialization into language, culture, and skills as well as their hetero-gendering and hetero-sexualization) are not only regulated by public norms and institutions, but also co-produce the public in its androcentric, racist and classist normativity, its border controls, its exclusions.

. . . and the State's Desire?

However, Queer Theory alone has consistently posed the question of the relevance of desire for installing and reproducing a binary-gendered and hetero-sexualized sphere of the political. Here I am not only talking about "the public," about a cultural sphere, or civil society; I would also like to draw attention to the organizing principles of political institutions, of the legal field, of capitalist processes, and forms of citizenship. Even nation-building can be analyzed, as Jacqui Alexander (1994) does in the case of postcolonial Bahamas, demonstrating its dependence on a dialectical heterosexualization of state-institutions and gendered subjectivities. She points out how state-politics serve a heterosexualized tourist industry while safeguarding patriarchal violence and homophobic abjection. Similarly Davina Cooper (2002) exposes the "sexualized character of the state itself" when she maps state scholarship in lesbian and gay studies, and studies the image of the state in queer theory and activism. For her, the concept of "the desiring state" will be a main field of interest for future queer studies. She points out three main aspects of this research yet-to-come: first of all "the way erotic energy can be found in projects and technologies of governance," secondly, "the extension of capitalist market relations within modern liberal states" (246), since they mobilize sexuality and desire, and, thirdly, a more explicit sexual citizenship that introduces erotic desires and intimacies into the public sphere. This last aspect seems to be the most provocative, but also the most hypothetical. Unfortunately, Cooper does not indicate how this might help to explain and democratize the state's desires.

Even though Nico Beger tends in the same direction when he focuses on "the desire for rights" as a driving force in l/g/b/t politics, he is more skeptical of its revolutionary effects. For him, desire induces political change while at the same times affirming hegemonic concepts of love, intimacy, and kinship; it never simply escapes the structuring force of heteronormativity: "Any analysis of rights politics needs to centralize desire as the motor of taking up oneself as a person belonging to a community in law or in social or political orders. Claiming rights becomes an appropriation of desire made relevant in the discourses of participation and citizenship, which are—among others—based on the regulatory practices of a gender order" (Beger 74). When Beger makes the concept of desire central to his analysis of l/g/b/t and queer politics in the European Union, he does so because it enables him to connect "the desire for the expression of one's sexuality and gender and the desire for equal rights" (71) as equally and interconnectedly constituting politics. Desire here is to be understood as an outcome of discursive practices and unconscious processes. As such it is productive of social realities, including identities, and it connects subjectivity and politics.

Shane Phelan does not use the concept of desire in her discussion of "queering citizenship." But when she votes for the end of the "phallic citizen" she implicitly reminds us that this phallic citizen relies on a notion of desire that nourishes his (?!) illusion of self-sufficiency by engaging women/other as his affirming mirror (Phelan 159). Instead of rescuing desire from its phallocentric function Phelan uses the term "passion" to promote her project of queering citizenship. Like Cooper, she opens up the idea that passions are not absent from governance and state policies, though they are denied by a supposedly rational and neutral liberal state. This works so well, because especially "the passions of adhesion—love (whether homosocial, familial, sexual, or all of these), empathy, desire" (Phelan 160) are delegated to the realm of the private. Therefore, Phelan suggests that we make explicit the hidden passions in public policies, that we problematize them and introduce these privatized "adhesive passions" into the public.

Even though I find this a provocative move that holds the possibility of challenging established norms and stereotypes, I am nevertheless skeptical about Phelan's idealistic understanding of love, empathy and desire. First of all, she runs the danger of condemning or devaluing all distancing or aggressive passions as well as sexual or kinship-relations that include anger, fear and hate in their repertoire. Also, she overestimates the transformative power of compassion over conflict. Thus she reproduces a gendered binary of "masculine" and "feminine" passions, which, even if she puts them in inverted commas, create an opposition of a "masculine state" versus a promising "queer community." The latter is idealistically characterized as "capable of acknowledging and thriving on the adhesive passions, using them to overcome fears and angers that have been signature passions of our times" (Phelan 160). In my opinion it seems more desirable to affirm contradictory and conflictual movements and to find non-violent ways to live them rather than to try to overcome them altogether.

Desire as Method?

All the above suggestions make it clear that it is not adequate to simply break up the public/private divide if it means that we gain access to the public only under the conditions of an ongoing heterosexualized superiority or a universal capitalist logic. Rather, the challenge is to rework the public so that it may embrace formerly privatized practices of reproduction, sexuality, intimacy, as well as to fight hierarchies, exclusions or normative inclusions, covert or overt? normalizations, and violence. How far does Probyn's suggestion of understanding "desire as a method" support this task? Why is it interesting for her to think about desire's methods? Why does she insist, that desire is not a metaphor but a method?

If we consult *Webster's International Dictionary* we learn that a "method" is a "procedure or process for attaining an object. . . a systematic procedure, technique, or set of rules employed in philosophical inquiry. . . a way, technique, or process for doing something. . . a body of skills and techniques." According to these definitions, what is convincing about "methods" is that they can be used to solve theoretical as well as practical problems. They might even transform into a "strategy" for reaching a political goal if we call the goal an "object." Thus, looking at Probyn's aim to use desire as a method, one can show how this enables her to combine analysis and anticipation within the same process. To figure out variable relations on social surfaces also means to create new images of the social as well as to anticipate a different future. Desire, if we recapitulate Probyn's view, is a productive force that works as a movement. It travels in images and creates connections between words and things and bodies.

Accordingly, to understand desire as a method means "to put desire to work in lines of flight, lines that scramble the subjective, the sexual, the social." To use this method as "a theoretical strategy, and a mode of cultural criticism" (62) means to engage and be engaged by desire, to "write within the engagement of desire [and to be] beyond interpretation. . . that seek[s] the origin of meaning" (61). Instead, one seeks for becomings and for new lines of flight.

Explicitly, Probyn mentions that she is not interested in just any kind of desire, but specifically seeks queer desire: a desire that cannot be defined by classificatory logic, that cannot be essentialized within individuals, but (to use a Deleuzian term) spreads itself over things: a desire traveling in queer images, creating queer images. Though:

> To be absolutely clear about it, the image is queer not in and of itself but in relation to other images and bodies—a movement that refuses to be policed at the same time that it says come to me, as it bends the line, causing changed relations of proximity. (60)

Does this become useful for macro-political analysis and socio-structural transformations? Central to Probyn's task is the question of how social categories translate into singularity. Social categories like race, class, and gender, the "zones of difference" available and enforced by a certain society, define the "specificity" of a certain context. They define the position from where lines of flight can evolve, they propose certain directions, certain speeds, certain modes of transportation; yet, they never endanger the contingency of desire's movement:

> The movement from specificity to singularity can be understood as processes that render the virtual actual—the ways in which the general becomes realized by individuals as singular. Simply put, we do not live our lives as categories: as a lesbian I should do this; as a feminist I ought to do that. (22)

To "render the virtual actual" also means that there is no clear-cut distinction between desire as a theoretical and as a practical method; to think singularity without referring to identity models or classificatory logic is a way of making connections that can be actualized in texts, and thoughts, as well as in practices and social relations. I find it very convincing that Probyn's method is simultaneously theoretical as well as practical, discursive as well as material, personal as well as social. But it seems to me, concerning the question of singularity, one should not so easily give up on a movement in the other direction: to render the actual virtual. The task would hereby be to create "specificities" that condition the way singularities relate and intersect, without reactivating a logic of classification and exclusion.

If we try to understand and transform institutions, formalized and legally regulated processes, governance and state practices, it can be useful to strengthen singularities in order to subvert the rule of institutionalized or hegemonic power, but it also seems to be necessary to know how specificities are constituted, secured, and reproduced. Of course, we can point out how specificities are rendered singular, and how in this process they produce unforeseen effects and assemblages. But assemblages are not necessarily dynamic formations: they stabilize and become hegemonic. This would mean turning the coin around and asking how singularities transform into specificities. Not only from an analytical but also from a transformative point of view it is interesting to know how singularities interact as forces in power relations and form specificities. Political activism that aims to intervene on a structural level cannot simply break up specificities into singularities and celebrate their contingent relations without taking up the "contingent necessity" to produce closures and to decide what exactly it "desires" to enforce.

Politics means that even if I know that I cannot overcome the arbitrariness of my own perspective, decisions have to be made—decisions which in the political arena are decisions that concern others—and, most probably upset others, provoke others, enrage others. If we do want to understand desire as a force of social transformation and not give away the chance to "design" public space and socio-political processes we not only have to ask how specificity translates into singularity, but also how we want singularity to translate into specificity.

"How we want"—another question of desire. Here again, Probyn might offer desire as a mobilizing force and images as modes of transportation. Images create assemblages of and in public spaces, assemblages which are singular even if they desire specificity. Therefore, in every single instance we would have to ask how queer resistance against identity categories and normative classifications produces material-semiotic effects on social surfaces: Do these effects shatter traditional value systems, scandalize? social inequalities and rearrange hierarchies? Do they irritate well-established, hegemonic habits? Do they subvert institutionalized versions of heterosexuality and binary gender arrangements? And then it might just turn out that we perceive new productive movements: private desires spill over into the public sphere; queer images connect with hegemonic practices; queer practices infuse images of the state.

Works Cited

Alexander, Jacqui M. "Erotic Autonomy as a Politics of Decolonization. An Anatomy of Feminist and State Practice in the Bahamas Tourist Economy." *Feminist Genealogies, Colonial Legacies, Democratic Futures*. Ed. Jacqui

M. Alexander and Chandra Talpade Mohanty. London: Routledge, 1997. 63-100.

Beger, Nico. Que(e)rying Political Practices in Europe: Tensions in the Struggle for Sexual Minority Rights. Amsterdam: ASCA, 2001.

Cooper, Davina. "Imagining the Place of the State: Where Governance and Social Power Meet." *Handbook of Gay and Lesbian Studies*. Ed. Diane Richardson and Steven Seidman. London: SAGE, 2002. 231-252.

Deleuze, Gilles. "Desire & Pleasure." *Globe E-Journal of Contempory Art* 5 (1997). Trans. Melissa McMahon <http://www.arts.monash.edu.au/visarts/globe/issue5/delfou.html>.

———, and Fèlix Guattari. *A Thousand Plateaus: Capitalism and Schizophrenia.* Trans. Brian Massumi. Minnesota: University of Minnesota Press, 1987.

———. *What is Philosophy?* New York: Columbia University Press, 1996.

Foucault, Michel. *The History of Sexuality, Volume I.* Harmondsworth: Penguin, 1981.

———. "Maurice Blanchot: The Thought from the Outside." *Foucault/Blanchot*. Trans. Brian Massumi. New York: Zone Books, 1987.

———. "Sexual Discourse and Power." *Culture and Society: Contemporary Debates.* Ed. Jeffrey Alexander and Steven Seidman. Cambridge: Cambridge UP, 1990.

Gregson, N. and G. Rose. "Taking Butler Elsewhere: Performativities, Spatialities and Subjectivities." *Environment and Planning D: Society and Space* 18 (2000): 433-452.

Hennessy, Rosemary. Profit and Pleasure: Sexual Identities in Late Capitalism. New York: Routledge, 2000.

Phelan, Shane. Sexual Strangers, Gays, Lesbians, and Dilemmas of Citizenship. Philadelphia: Temple Press, 2001.

Probyn, Elspeth: *Outside Belongings*. London: Routledge, 1996.

Valentine, Gill. "Queer Bodies and the Production of Space." *Handbook of Gay and Lesbian Studies.* Ed. Diane Richardson and Steven Seidman. London: SAGE, 2002: 145-160.

Webster's Third New International Dictionary. London: MacMillan, 1971.

HANDLING THE TOUCHY SUBJECT: DEALING WITH THE AUTHOR'S ALLEGED OR ACTUAL HOMOSEXUALITY IN POLISH STUDIES IN THE HISTORY OF ENGLISH LITERATURE

KRZYSZTOF FORDOŃSKI

Literary studies is one of those fields of research in the humanities where the issue of homosexuality may appear especially visible. On the one hand, there are queer theory specialists who deal with camp or queer elements in texts; on the other, the issue appears in the study of the authors' biographies. While scholars may choose whether or not to discuss the camp element of a text or do a queer reading, an objective presentation of an author's biography (should such a presentation constitute a part of the scholarly study) is a duty which goes beyond discussion.

Even a cursory glance at anthologies or studies in the history of English literature proves that scholars take a variety of approaches to this duty when homosexual or homoerotic elements appear in the presented biographies of writers. Even those scholars who feel perfectly free to describe the sexual promiscuity of writers become silent when such activities concern people of the same sex. We may also find contrary examples when scholars use the opportunity to present their own views on the subject, occasionally going so far as to make even remotely possible homosexual behavior the focal point of their biographical studies and literary analyses. Such authors seem to forget Jacob Stockinger's warning that "ignoring historical, social, and artistic realities, this kind of minority criticism ends up being evaluative rather than cognitive and risks turning first-rate authors into second-rate ideologues or vice-versa" (Crew 135). As the following study demonstrates, this danger does not seem too imminent for Polish scholars.

The purpose of the present study is to analyze the image of homosexuality in English literature as presented in thirteen existing works on English literature and its history published in Poland (including one translation). The selected works are general studies in or anthologies of English literature which include biographical information.

Quite obviously, this does not mean that these Polish studies have been used as the only teaching materials available. To point out the schizophrenia caused (though probably not realized by most lecturers) by the usage of Polish and American or British handbooks Polish versions shall be contrasted with foreign ones in discussion of specific biographies, wherever the discrepancies are especially glaring. The two most popular and generally available *Oxford* and *Norton Anthology of English Literature* shall provide a point of reference here.

The study shall begin with a general presentation of each of the works discussed, the importance of the biographical element in each book, its underlying assumptions, and reception. This part shall be complemented with specific examples taken from the biographies of ten British authors whose alleged or actual homosexuality is most often discussed. A remark should be made at this point that the number of references does not necessarily reflect the interest of Polish scholars in the life of a given author as the works in question differ greatly in the time span they cover.

Another necessary remark is that the English authors selected for this study are all men. The initial idea was to use as examples an equal number of men and women As it turned out, however, the presented studies seem to echo the anecdote about queen Victoria who allegedly personally ordered lesbian sex to be removed from the list of sexual activities criminalized by the Contagious Disease Act. Among the works discussed below the only source to mention the existence of such writers as Radclyffe Hall, Virginia Woolf or Jeanette Winterson is Sikorska 1996. Otherwise, sex between women does not seem to exist in English literature as seen by Polish academics.

The present study attempts to reconstruct the image of homosexuality a student or a reader interested in literature may arrive at after reading the discussed books. The study may also serve as an attempt to reconstruct the changes in attitudes towards homosexuality held among English literature scholars in Poland over the presented period. It does not attempt to answer the question whether the discussed authors actually were homosexual, gay or bisexual (however anachronistic all the terms actually are in reference to people living before the 19th century when these terms were formulated), we shall follow here Diana Fuss's suggestion "we cannot know—surely or definitely. . . if one is gay" (Fuss 6). Metaphorically speaking, we discuss here the mirrors and the, quite probably, distorted image they offer, not the objects they reflect.

* * *

The list of works under discussion starts with the two volume selection of *Specimens of English Poetry and Prose* edited by Stanisław Helsztyński (1954) reprinted nine times until 1986. The book was by far the most popular English literature handbook in Poland until the late 1980s when English and American anthologies became more widely available. Its introductory notes seldom exceed one page of which the biography usually takes up one or two paragraphs. The sources consulted were, in most cases, published before World War II, which partly explains the absolute chastity of this work.

The second work under discussion is Margaret Schlauch's *English Medieval Literature and Its Social Foundations* published in 1956. Although usually quite well informed in matters of the personal lives of the writers, this work does not include any information on the authors' homosexuality or any other sexual behaviour.

In 1967, George Sampson's *The Concise Cambridge History of English Literature* was published in the Polish translation by Piotr Graff. The Polish title, *Historia literatury angielskiej w zarysie: Podręcznik*, clearly indicated that this publication was meant as a handbook for Polish students of English literature, a claim which was further supported by an introduction by Margaret Schlauch. First published in 1941 and updated slightly for the 1961 edition, this book presents an extremely prudish approach to biographical matters. The author's attitude is apparent in the chapter on Burns: "A history of literature is not concerned with the private lives of poets, unless the lives offer elucidations of the poems" (595). Although Sampson's goal of achieving objectivity deserves praise (especially but not exclusively as far as homosexuality is concerned), he assumes that the reader does not need to be informed about the author's life at all. The turbulent emotional life of Robert Burns which so greatly influenced his work therefore deserves only half a sentence: "Everywhere he found companions of his own sex with whom he joined in clubs for debating, as well as friends of the other sex about whom he wrote verses" (Sampson, *The Concise* 596).

The next two books under discussion supplemented the selection provided by Stanisław Helsztyński which ends with high Victorian literature. *English Poetry of the Twentieth Century* (1979) by Wanda Rulewicz and *English Poetry of the Nineteenth Century* (1980) by Wanda Krajewska both include comprehensive biographical notes (two to three pages each) which are further supplemented by critical commentaries on specific works. Even though the biographies include rather detailed descriptions of the poets' love lives, for instance of Wordsworth's French affair (Krajewska 29), the presence of the homosexual element is limited to one or two allusions in each of the works.

"Literatura angielska" (English Literature), a chapter written in 1982 by Henryk Zbierski for the second volume of Władysław Floryan's *Dzieje literatur europejskich*, was the first originally Polish comprehensive study of the history of English Literature. Zbierski presents biographical notes of very different length and usually omits any allusions to sexual behaviour.

Powieść angielska XX wieku (English Novel of the 20th Century) by Bronisława Bałutowa, a study in the development of the English novel published in 1983, presents quite lengthy biographical notes which abound in very personal information about the novelists. However, the overtly homosexual writers are treated with an attitude bordering on homophobia, which is especially visible in the case of Christopher Isherwood (118-120).

Historia literatury angielskiej: Zarys (History of English Literature: An Outline) by Przemysław Mroczkowski (1986) is characterised by a mellifluous and highly ornamental style, but the biographical materials included in this study seldom touch upon the more delicate aspects of writers' biographies regardless of their sexual preferences.

The very personal selection of poetic translations by Stanisław Barańczak in *Od Chaucera do Larkina: 400 nieśmiertelnych wierszy 125 poetów anglojęzycznych z 8 stuleci* (From Chaucer to Larkin: 400 Immortal Poems of 125 English-Language Poets from 8 Centuries) (1993) was supplemented by short biographical notes including general descriptions of the literary style and achievement of a given author. They do not allude to any non-normative sexual preferences of the poets.

An Outline History of English Literature by Liliana Sikorska (1996), includes biographical notes of unequal length, ranging from a few lines or dates to essays consisting of several pages. The author is by far the most courageous in presenting the writers' homosexuality and discusses numerous literary works of homoerotic character.

In 1997, Zbigniew Mazur and Teresa Bela published *The College Anthology of English Literature* which, as the title suggest, is primarily a selection of texts intended for students of teacher training colleges. Introductory notes supplement every chapter presenting the major works of a given literary epoch. Specific information about the discussed authors consists mostly of dates of birth and death, in some cases the notes include the titles of their most important works and short descriptions of their literary achievement.

Liliana Sikorska and Jacek Fabiszak published *An Anthology of English Literature. From Beowulf to John Milton* in 1998. Their concise biographical notes apart from absolutely basic data provide only titles of works and dates of their creation or publication. The second volumes *From the Restoration Age through Romanticism* by Gerard Nawrocki was published in 1999. The two volumes include more detailed notes (on the average one page).

* * *

The list of English writers whose actual or alleged homosexuality is subject to discussion in a study of literature must begin with the still debatable case of William Shakespeare. Any suggestions concerning the alleged homosexuality of Shakespeare (a married man with three children) are based exclusively upon the descriptions of his tender feelings toward an anonymous young man in *The Sonnets* and the volume's mysterious dedication. The first to mention the issue was George Sampson who dealt with the question very briefly and unhesitatingly: "Neither dedication nor commentary has any real importance for the lover of poetry. They appeal to the wrong kind of curiosity" (*The Concise* 271).

Polish sources, though quite numerous, generally omit the issue. Henryk Zbierski in his chapter "Literatura angielska" only hints at certain psychological truth of the experience presented in the collection: "It is especially important that the subject of psychological analyses in *The Sonnets* is no longer a fictitious character but an authentic person and a poet—William Shakespeare himself" ("Literatura angielska" 386). It was only six years later that Zbierski faced the allegations in his monographic study about William Shakespeare and rejected them as follows:

> If we exclude from our analyses Shakespeare's alleged homosexuality, as we are entitled to do not only due to a complete lack of any extra-literary proofs or circumstances but also because of the poet's own conscious rejection of any such accusations (Sonnet XX), the only possible explanation is the fact that the love towards a young man expressed in so many different ways is 'the heavenly love' described by Plato in his *Symposium*. (*William Shakespeare* 552-553)

Sikorska echoes these statements (though she clearly takes sides in the dispute concerning the name of the addressee of the collection), arguing that:

> the sonnets are not the celebration of ideal love for a woman; rather they render the affection of an older man towards a young man. The supposed homosexual love between Shakespeare and Herbert has never been truly proved. It is rather a clear reference to the classical Platonic love between two men. (86)

The biography of Christopher Marlowe provides much more data concerning his homosexuality. Polish scholars, however, prefer not to discuss the issue, as did Helsztyński writing that of Marlowe's "life after he left the University almost nothing is known" (249). Mroczkowski only adds that "the uncontrollable Christopher mingled with free-thinkers of greatly provocative opinions" (150).

Zbierski does not provide a longer biographical note for Marlowe. However, he comments (mainly upon *Edward II* and the allusion becomes clear only to readers familiar with the text of the play) that "the difference between Marlowe and Shakespeare as well as Kyd and other Elizabethan playwrights is his lyrical engagement which makes his tragedies largely a projection of his personality" ("Literatura angielska" 350).

Fabiszak is the most open of the critics whose studies include presentations of the works and life of Christopher Marlowe. However, he also prefers a roundabout way of bringing up the delicate subject: "Marlowe's early and untimely death was a result of his notorious and adventurous conduct which did not go unnoticed. . . . After his death various charges were brought against him by, amongst others, his friends: Thomas Kyd and Richard Baines. Marlowe was accused of blasphemy, atheism and homosexuality" (Sikorska 273 and 358—the same note).

George Gordon Noel Lord Byron was characterised by Harold Bloom and Lionel Trilling as follows:

> A virtual synonym for the greatest of lovers, he was passive towards women, sodomistic, sado-masochistic, fundamentally homosexual, and early disgusted with all sexual experience anyway. Outcast for his incest with his half-sister, he nevertheless seems to have gotten beyond narcissistic self-regard only in relation to her, yet she was in no way remarkable. . . . [In Greece] he found a last bitter, frustrated homosexual passion for his page boy Loukas, and his final verses and letters betray profound self-disgust. (285-286)

The Norton Anthology of English Literature edited by M. H. Abrams is much less direct suggesting only that "Byron seems to have had one attribute in common with the Byronic hero—a compulsion to try forbidden experience (including, as we now know, homosexual love affairs) joined with a tendency to court his own destruction" (505). Most Polish authors prefer not to mention these elements of his biography at all. Sampson, however, in his typically prudish way writes about the reasons of Byron's exile from Great Britain: "A history of literature is no place for the succulent discussion of scandal. Lady Byron herself accused him of nothing but insanity" (*The Concise* 627). This somehow does not stop him from supplying further the essentials of this unfortunate affair.

Krajewska commenting upon Byron's choice of self-exile adds only that "he was also suspected of homosexuality" (118). Barańczak remarks upon his "rampant and rather risky sexual life (including an affair with his half-sister)" (291) while Mazur and Bela quite atypically for their otherwise extremely concise presentation note that: "Byron and Shelley held unorthodox views on religion and morality, expressed both in their poetry and in their lives, which many of their contemporaries found shocking and unacceptable" (367). Neither editor clarifies what specifically was so shocking about Byron's views upon morality as his attitude towards religion was quite orthodox and the poet was himself shocked by the atheist free-thinking expressed by Shelley (Bloom 285).

Alfred Lord Tennyson's emotional life was, according to majority of his biographers, extremely dull. In 1830, he fell in love with Emily Sellwood, they became engaged in 1838, but the poet "could not marry, because of poverty, until 1850" (Abrams 1094). They lived happily ever after and Mrs Tennyson bore him two sons Hallam and Lionel.

Quite a different and rather surprising approach to Tennyson's life can be found in Bloom and Trilling:

> [Tennyson] entered Trinity College, Cambridge, in 1827, where he fell in love with Arthur Henry Hallam. . . . The friendship between the two was the most important experience of Tennyson's life, and if it had a repressed sexual element, neither Tennyson nor Hallam (nor anyone else) seems ever to have been aware of this. (1180)

Polish scholars do not follow this rather muddled presentation: a love or friendship—with an uncertain repressed sexual element—which went unnoticed by the two gentlemen supposedly involved as well as by everyone else. Nevertheless, quite a few authors felt a need to comment upon the feeling which is overtly called love in the collection *In Memoriam*. The approach is unequivocal: the feeling must have actually been friendship and consequently Helsztyński informs us that Tennyson "formed close friendship with Arthur Henry Hallam" (275), Krajewska states that of the poet's life's tragedies "the greatest was the early and sudden death of his best friend Hallam" (52) while Zbierski notices that *In Memoriam* was written "on the occasion of the death of a very close friend of the poet, A. H. Hallam" ("Literatura angielska" 500).

Gerard Manley Hopkins' homosexuality is generally seldom mentioned. Therefore, it does not seem surprising that only one Polish source mentions the fact in passing. Sikorska suggests that "some of [Hopkins'] obscurity might have to do with his homosexual orientation, which seems to underlie his most personal poems" (236-237) which is presented in much closer detail in *The Oxford Anthology*:

> Hopkins underwent a [religious] crisis, which came in March 1865 and resulted from meeting an enthusiastic, very young, and beautiful religious poet, Digby Dolben, who was to drown in June 1867 at the age of nineteen. That Hopkins fell in love with Dolben is quite likely, and it is also possible that his subsequent ascetic revulsion away from the world was, on an unconscious level, a revulsion away from his own desires. (1466)

The question of homosexuality so profoundly influenced the life of Oscar Wilde that it seems absolutely impossible to omit it even in the shortest presentation of his biography. Sampson rather peevishly speaks about Wilde's tragic overthrow of which "*The Ballad of Reading Gaol* (1898) and the unconvincing *De Profundis* (1905) are the product" (*The Concise* 845) but he fails to clarify what caused such a tragic end of the career.

All other sources are much more explicit about Wilde's tragic end. Zbierski presents the affair rather briefly: "Queensbury caused the downfall of Wilde [provoking the trial] as an effect of which Wilde was sentenced to two years hard labour for practising homosexuality" ("Literatura angielska" 519), concluding further that as a result of "his downfall—demeaning in the eyes of almost all the contemporary society—the rules he preached were, at least for a time, brought into disrepute. Wilde was therefore a disputable ally for modernity and the 'modern'" ("Literatura angielska" 520).

Bałutowa mentions Wilde only in her introduction in a similar vein, explaining predominance of realistic traits in the twentieth century English novel as follows: "Aestheticism in England was soon gone (mainly due to the scandalous trial of Oscar Wilde who was considered a typical product of the epoch)" (13).

Mroczkowski presents the affair in a few words but this sparks a rather long presentation of a very personal, hardly justified and quite ridiculous approach to the writer and his influence upon modern morals in general:

> Perhaps it was the instinct [of self-preservation] that Wilde lacked when his close friendship with Lord Alfred Douglas changed into a homosexual affair. . . . It is not clear whether more fuss was made by the circles in England of those days which condemned Wilde's (a married man's) behaviour or those circles which castigated the persecutors. The law of action and reaction is evidently at work here. The contemporary elimination of sense of responsibility in sexual matters which is on the increase and the general indulgence in the West in all kinds of behaviour seem to be the final stage of evolution which began in those days by affairs such as that of Wilde. All this does not change another aspect of the whole affair: the pitiless attitude of the society towards a person found as sinful or lost, a person well known for his kind heart." (485-486)

Sikorska initially seems to pinpoint boredom as the reason for Wilde's homosexuality: "Wilde married. . . had two sons, and after three years, got bored and started having affairs with men" (240). In her commentary upon *The Picture of Dorian Gray* she further reflects that the novel "contains hints of the homosexual relationship between Dorian and his friend, the painter Basil Hallward, yet nothing is ever expressly voiced in the book" (241). The conclusions of the chapter, however, are more serious and may be among the best informed passages concerning the homosexuality of an English writer in Polish scholarly works:

Homosexual eros is implicit in the nature of Wilde's exploration of the relationship between body and mind as the route to self-knowledge revealed in the early poetry (Behrendt 1991:12). In 1866, the Contagious Disease Act was passed; it was a political act that threatened prostitution as well as homosexuality as diseases. Up till that point homosexuality was connected with sodomy and felony (in 1533 it was a capital offence punishable by death). Wilde himself was imprisoned for homosexuality. When in jail, he wrote a long letter to Lord Alfred Douglas, in which he revealed the nature of their relationships and chronicled the effect prison had on him. (242-243)

Bronisława Bałutowa's comments upon Edward Morgan Forster end with the conclusion that "the posthumously published early novel of Foster, *Maurice* (1971) was an interesting work for Forster's biographers, mainly due to the fact that it clearly confirms what had not been a mystery—Forster's homosexuality" (81). Forster's homosexuality actually was a mystery even for most of his critics, as can be seen from reviews of *Maurice* while the novel was, in fact, Forster's penultimate work followed and overshadowed by *A Passage to India*. From this revealing statement Bałutowa moves on, however, to more general conclusions drawn from the fact of the writer's homosexuality which:

> decidedly influenced certain motifs present in his works: love between a man and a woman is usually presented rather blandly, unconvincingly; the young women are most often not too agreeable, they are presented from an ironical distance, while older women—as Ruth Wilcox in *Howards End* and Mrs Moore in *A Passage to India* are idealised symbols of maternal fondness, human love, wisdom of the heart. Forster depicts most vividly the subtleties of friendship among men; this is especially visible in the relationship (kept within the boundaries of pure friendship) of Aziz and Fielding. (81-82)

Sikorska echoes only the first part of Bałutowa's evaluation, stating that: "Forster's last novel, published posthumously in 1971 is *Maurice*. It is a rather negligible work but for certain allusions which clearly prove Forster's homosexuality" (288). Other sources do not mention either the fact of Forster's homosexuality or the existence of *Maurice*.

Wystan Hugh Auden's homosexuality seems the most difficult to swallow for Polish scholars. Auden's friend Christopher Isherwood is mentioned only in two sources, both of which take very similar stand towards his post-war, overtly homosexual works. The camp element present in his earlier works, especially in *Goodbye to Berlin*, which Isherwood himself discussed in his 1976 memoir *Christopher and His Kind*, clearly escaped critical attention, as did Isherwood's later memoirs. Bronisława Bałutowa concentrates on praising his pre-war works, suggesting he was "intellectually more subtle than Graham Greene" (120), but in her opinion Isherwood "unlike Green, could not adapt to the changing times with their contemporary problems. . . . His post-war work. . . echoes the moods and view of the thirties. Modernity is only superficially sketched by the introduction of drastic sexual descriptions or the propagation of homosexuality as an appropriate kind of rebellion against bourgeois morality" (120).

Not surprisingly, Bałutowa fails to mention in her study of Graham Greene (106-113) his collection of erotic and also homoerotic short stories *May We Borrow Your Husband, Poppy?* Sikorska generally echoes these evaluations (choosing the same novel by Isherwood as her example) stating that "His post-war writing, like *Meeting by the River* (1967) shows an interest in Hindu philosophy but is not as ingenious as his pre-war pieces" (295). It is remarkable that the title of the most important post-war novel by Christopher Isherwood *A Single Man* (1964) is not mentioned in any Polish commentaries.

* * *

The choice of quotations chosen for this study may seem biased. To avoid such accusations I have attempted to include all references to the sexuality of the selected authors that can be found in the discussed anthologies, even when actual connection of such references with homosexuality may be disputable. The resulting impression may thus seem exaggerated but this is mainly because without quoting extensively it is impossible to demonstrate what a small part of the notes in question these opinions form. Similarly, a more detailed comparison between the discussion of "straight" emotional lives of writers and their gay counterparts would require too much space. I can only hope that the small number of quotations found on thousands of pages speaks for itself.

Naturally, the list of discussed names could be expanded but this would not significantly alter the conclusions of the present article. Neither of the presented Polish scholars ever mentions the sexual preferences of A. E. Housman, Wilfred Owen, Charles Algernon Swinburne, Thom Gunn or Philip Larkin, who could also classify as "alleged or actual homosexuals."

These examples indicate that from the 1950s to the 1970s the question of homosexuality was not raised in Polish anthologies of English literature. The first shifts in attitude can be traced to the early 1980s, when scholars no longer felt bound to remain silent but neither were yet bound by political correctness to refrain from expressing more or less veiled homophobic evaluations. Recent studies tend to discuss the issue more thoroughly though sexuality still seems much less interesting than other aspects of private lives of the writers.

Oddly enough, from the quotations provided above it becomes apparent that Polish literary critics are much more open to issues of sexuality when they write in English, which means that their works are addressed quite exclusively to

University students. None of the Polish language works (with the rather notorious exception of Bałutowa) which are intended for a wider audience risks any allusions to homosexuality. The only departure from the general rule is the treatment of Oscar Wilde, whose homosexuality is more freely discussed by scholars, perhaps because they consider this to be absolutely necessary.

Eve Kosofsky Sedgwick in her *Epistemology of the Closet* presented a sequence of eight dismissals which are usually offered as answers to any doubts concerning the sexuality of authors (when answers such as "Don't ask" or "You shouldn't know" are no longer sufficient). Polish scholars (at least in the works addressed to students or the general public rather than to fellow scholars) do not resort to all the strategies of dismissal yet their attitudes coincide with the range of approaches presented by Segdwick, especially with the three final options:

> 6. The author under discussion is certified or rumoured to have had an attachment to someone of the other sex—so their feelings about people of their own sex must have been completely meaningless. Or (under a perhaps somewhat different rule of admissible evidence)
> 7. There is no actual proof of homosexuality, such as sperm taken from the body of another man or a nude photograph with another woman—so the author may be assumed to have been ardently and exclusively heterosexual. Or (as a last resort)
> 8. The author or the author's important attachments may very well have been homosexual—but it would be provincial to let so insignificant a fact make any difference at all to our understanding of any serious project of life, writing, or thought. (52-53)

Their application in Poland chronologically follows the pattern proposed by Segdwick. The attitude changed from using all available counter-arguments to reject any possibility of an author's homosexuality to (prevailing at the moment) unwilling acceptance of the fact (at least whenever it is impossible to deny it). Such an acceptance, however, is not followed by ascribing to the fact any importance whatsoever. It is curious enough that as it can be seen from the quotations provided earlier on, the critics often seem obliged to "excuse" the discussed authors for who they were and what they did.

The image of homosexuality in English literature that a student or admirer of the literature can get from the discussed sources may be quite difficult to reconstruct. Some readers may not be able to reconstruct any image at all. The selection provided above is the result of a close reading of thirteen sources. Many of the allusions in the excerpts provided above reveal their meaning only after one reads the works referred to, which are seldom included in reading lists and are difficult to obtain either in English or in Polish translation. The realistic conclusion is therefore that students of English literature who limit their studies to Polish sources would not notice any role or even presence of homosexuality in English literature but for the notorious exception of Oscar Wilde. Polish readers forced by the lack of a working knowledge of English to limit themselves to Polish language studies and translations of literary works, would inevitably come to the same conclusion.

Is an almost graphic openness such as that presented in *Oxford Anthology of English Literature* the most advisable solution? A reasonable middle way should probably be advised for future authors of academic handbooks of English literature who would choose to include biographical studies in their work. They should be aware of the fact that the subject is no longer truly touchy and deserves a complete and objective presentation even from scholars who disapprove of homosexuality on moral grounds.

When scholars decide to introduce homosexual issues in their field of study they should nevertheless take into consideration Jakob Stockinger's commentaries given in his article "Homotextuality: A Proposal":

> [there is a] kind of bias in criticism [which] is a blend of commendable intentions and questionable methods. Certain critics, amateurs and professionals alike, focus on minority sexuality in literature from the viewpoint of the author, not the text. The notion of the "biographical phallacy" proved long ago that an easy and self-evident proportion cannot necessarily be established between a writer and his writings. There are of course intimate and casual ties between the two, but they are much more subtle and intricate than it is usually suggested by critics who treat fiction as merely literary transpositions of biographical facts. This approach can be valuable in that at least it opens up the issue of minority sexuality to critical enquiry; but it fails to the degree it falls into the very traps set out by formalists to demonstrate the textual impertinency of minority criticism. Applied judiciously, the approach certainly merits a place in critical methods—authors like Gide and Genet, who readily admit a close relationship between their works and themselves, seem particularly suited to minimizing the errors of the technique—but even in the most favourable cases, its use must remain as limited as its results. (Crew 137)

If any prescription should stem from the present study, which was clearly conceived as a case study with little prescriptive purpose, it must be based upon the fundamental question whether an awareness of an author's biography is essential, necessary or at least advisable for the study of literature. To put it in other words—we need to ask ourselves whether Sampson's approach is completely erroneous. Should the answer to this basic question be affirmative, it seems obvious that the treatment of any element of biography must not be influenced either by the scholar's personal approach or by fear of "tackling a touchy subject" or abusing some vaguely defined moral standards. Studies of literature offer a wide of range of approaches which exclude the author completely from the field of critical interest. The choice to examine a writer's biography or to leave it out is therefore free but once a critic decides to select for his or her studies an author whose life may be treated by some as a touchy subject, he or she ought to follow one general policy—that of honesty.

Notes

1. The quotations given in the text of this article are taken from the English original, specifically from the 1961 edition which was used for Polish translation. In all other cases English translations of quotations provided in the text are by the present author.
2. Reissued in 2002 as *Historia literatury angielskiej* in a separate volume. Page numbers in this text refer to the original 1982 edition.
3. Originally published in 1978 in two volumes as *Zarys historii literatury angielskiej*. The 1986 edition used for the present study combined the two volumes the text of which was slightly extended. It was reprinted at least once in the 1990s.
4. An enlarged and corrected edition appeared in 2002. The quotations in this article were taken from the original edition.
5. Zbierski thus joins a long line of scholars who use Shakespeare's Sonnet XX as a proof of his homo- or heterosexuality. For a presentation of this debate see: Woods 1998: 104-106.
6. The Polish translator preferred to soften this statement by putting the word "insane" in inverted commas (*Historia literatury* 696).
7. The quotation comes from P. F. Behrendt, *Oscar Wilde: Eros and Aesthetics*. New York: St Martin Press, 1991.
8. See: Gardner 433-489.
9. Only in the case of Shakespeare (as it can be seen from the quotations from Zbierski and Sikorska provided above) and to a lesser extent in the case of Marlowe can we find instances of dismissal: "Passionate language of same-sex attraction was extremely common during whatever period is under discussion—and therefore must have been completely meaningless" (Sedgwick 52).

Works Cited

Abrams, M. H., ed. *The Norton Anthology of English Literature*. Fifth Edition. Volume 2. New York, London: W. W. Norton & Company, 1986.
Bałutowa, Bronisława. *Powieść angielska XX wieku*. Warszawa: Państwowe Wydawnictwo Naukowe, 1983.
Barańczak, Stanisław. Od Chaucera do Larkina. 400 nieśmiertelnych wierszy 125 poetów anglojęzycznych z 8 stuleci. Kraków: Wydawnictwo Znak. 1993.
Crew, Louie. *The Gay Academic*. Palm Springs: ETC Publications, 1978.
Fuss, Diana, ed. *Inside/Out: Lesbian Theory, Gay Theory*. New York: Routledge, 1991.

Gardner, Philip, ed. *E. M. Forster. The Critical Heritage.* London: Routledge & Kegan Paul, 1973.
Helsztyński, Stanisław. *Specimens of English Poetry and Prose.* 2 vols. Warszawa: Państwowe Wydawnictwo Naukowe, 1986.
Krajewska, Wanda. *English Poetry of the Nineteenth Century.* Warszawa: Państwowe Wydawnictwo Naukowe, 1980.
Mazur, Zbigniew & Teresa Bela. *The College Anthology of English Literature.* Kraków: Universitas, 1997.
Mroczkowski, Przemysław. *Historia literatury angielskie: Zarys.* Second Edition. Wrocław: Zakład Narodowy im. Ossolińskich, 1986.
Nawrocki, Gerard. An Anthology of English Literature: From the Restoration Age through Romanticism. Poznań: Dom Wydawniczy Rebis, 1999.
The Oxford Anthology of English Literature. Volume II 1800 to the Present. Eds. Harold Bloom and Lionel Trilling, Part 1. "Romantic Poetry and Prose." Lionel Trilling and Harold Bloom, Part 2. "Victorian Poetry and Prose." Frank Kermode and John Hollander, Part 3. "Modern British Literature." New York: Oxford University Press, 1973.
Rulewicz, Wanda. *English Poetry of the Twentieth Century.* Warszawa: Wydawnictwa Uniwersytetu Warszawskiego, 1979.
Sampson, George. *The Concise Cambridge History of English Literature.* Cambridge: Cambridge University Press, 1961.
———. *Historia literatury angielskiej w zarysie: Podręcznik.* Przekład z języka angielskiego Piotr Graff. Warszawa: Państwowe Wydawnictwo Naukowe, 1967.
Schlauch, Margaret. *English Medieval Literature and Its Social Foundations.* Warszawa: Państwowe Wydawnictwo Naukowe, 1956.
Sedgwick, Eve Kosofsky. *Epistemology of the Closet.* Berkeley, Los Angeles: University of California Press, 1990.
Sikorska. Liliana. *An Outline History of English Literature.* Poznań: Bene Nati, 1996.
———, and Jacek Fabiszak. An Anthology of English Literature: From Beowulf to John Milton. Poznań: Dom Wydawniczy Rebis, 1998.
Woods, Gregory. *A History of Gay Literature: The Male Tradition.* New Haven and London: Yale University Press, 1998.
Zbierski, Henryk. "Literatura angielska." *Dzieje literatur europejskich.* Vol. II Part 1. Ed. Władysław Floryan. Warszawa: Państwowe Wydawnictwo Naukowe, 1982.
———. *William Shakespeare.* Warszawa: Wiedza Powszechna, 1988.
———. *Historia literatury angielskiej.* Poznań: Oficyna Wydawnicza Atena, 2002.

TAMIL AND QUEER: POLITICAL AND SEXUAL MARGINALIZATION IN SHYAM SELVADURAI'S *FUNNY BOY*

ANNA BRANACH-KALLAS

Shyam Selvadurai's debut novel *Funny Boy* (1994) can be considered a "coming out novel" as it depicts the central protagonist's passage to maturity and sexual awakening and his acceptance of his homosexual orientation. It has been recognized as such by the literary establishment; winner of the W.H. Smith/Books in Canada First Novel Award and the Lambda Literary Award for Best Gay Men's Fiction, *Funny Boy* received immediate critical acclaim. However, the novel appears to be extremely complex in its portrayal of various forms of oppression and resistance; it focuses not only on the marginalization of sexual alterity but also on the exclusion of other ex-centric groups, such as women or ethnic minorities. *Funny Boy* depicts the mechanisms of micro-powers and macro-power, those discourses which, according to Michel Foucault, differentiate, hierarchize and exclude (Foucault, *Discipline* 183): the construction of heterosexuality through prohibition and coercion, the subjugation of women within patriarchal family, the coercive practices of disciplinary institutions such as the school, and finally the surveillance of the State which aims to protect its essential homogeneity. The protagonists of the novel, set in Sri Lanka in the 1970s and the 1980s, belong to the colonized upper middle class, a group defining gender roles through the typically Western binary opposition and following British models of appropriate conduct. The "norm" is therefore defined for them by Western gendered stereotypes, whereas the luxuriousness and transgression of vestimentary codes, traditionally associated with Southern Asia, falls outside the respectable and the prescribed.

The normative discourse that operates in the first chapter of the novel attempts to lock the protagonist, a small Sri Lankan boy, in a stereotypical gender position. However, from the very beginning, Arjie's resistance to these mechanisms of power is suggested by the narrator. Depicting the territorial division of his grandmother's property between boys and girls, Arjie observes that he has "gravitated naturally" (3) into the second category. Sexual transgression together with his vivid imagination give him the position of a leader among the girls of his family. Interestingly, the favorite game of this group is "bride-bride"—the performance of a wedding ceremony with the figure of the bride at the center. While playing the game, the children are acutely aware of gender roles; it is the bride that is the heroine of the performance, whereas the groom's territory is the office, which makes his role particularly unattractive. It is Arjie who plays the role of the bride, while the groom is impersonated by a girl. This example of cross-dressing illuminates the mobility of gender and resistance to normative sexual identity. Thus, Selvadurai illustrates Joan Riviere's classic assertion that womanliness can "be assumed and worn as a mask" (Riviere 38). What is more, Arjie emphasizes the game's potential for asserting his autonomy and liberation:

> The dressing of the bride would now begin, and then, by the transfiguration I saw taking place in Janaki's cracked full-length mirror—by the sari being wrapped around my body, the veil being pinned to my head, the rouge put on my cheeks, lipstick on my lips, kohl around my eyes—I was able to leave the constraints of myself and ascend into another, more brilliant, more beautiful self, a. . . perfect being upon whom the adoring eyes of the world rested. (4-5)

This act of transgression provokes in the dominant group severe opposition and immediate attempts to reassert the limits prescribed by the norm. Betrayed by an envious cousin, Arjie, disguised as a bride, has to face his relatives' mocking laughter and his father's anger. His behavior is deemed insufficiently "manly" but the boy does not understand the character of the subversion that he is accused of. He is punished by being forced to play cricket with the other boys of the family. When he protests against this punishment, Arjie is given such arguments as: "It's good for you" (19), "big boys must play with other boys" (20). His parents consider cricket as belonging to the domain of typically male sports, rituals of manhood that will force Arjie to identify with masculinity. For through shared activity, such as sport, the members of a group implicitly identify with one another and with ego ideals:

> Learning to be a man is learning to gain esteem through a form of self-presentation that associates one with deals of manhood. . . . When everyone in a group identifies with the same ego ideal, they identify with each other. (Beneke 70)

Thus, cricket represents what Timothy Beneke calls a *ritual of compulsive masculinity*, "a form of structured developmental emotion work in the service of gender" (Beneke 65). This is why the admission of Arjie, the "girlie-boy," into the team threatens its integrity. Arjie, perceived as belonging to the realm of the feminine, weakens the ties of male bonding between the members of the team.

Challenging the ideal of masculinity, Arjie puts into question the ego ideal that holds the group together. Insensitive to the appeals of his brother Diggy, captain of the team, who exclaims,"Come on, *men*!" (27; my emphasis), the boys will reaffirm their ties with the group only when Arjie is excluded from the team and prohibited to enter the world of male sports forever. Their violent reaction proves that male bonding is, in fact, characterized by intense homophobia. It is interesting that Arjie seems well aware of the mechanisms of male bonding, but he uses his knowledge to oppose the norm. Far from feeling humiliated by this act of exclusion, he pretends to accept the rules of proving manhood only in order to evade identification with it. Masculinity, like femininity, can be worn as a mask; masquerade provides again a strategy of subversion of the heterosexual construction of gender. What is more, by relegating the masculine to the area of the performative, *Funny Boy* illustrates the failure of a discourse of power to regulate individual conduct.

In the first chapter of the novel, Selvadurai also draws the reader's attention to the significance of naming in the construction of sexual identity. According to Judith Butler, our subjectivity is constructed through interpellation and thus the discursive act of naming acquires a performative function (see Butler, "Critically Queer"). Faced with Arjie's queerness, his relatives react by calling him "funny," "a pansy," "a faggot," "a sissy," "a girlie-boy," all more or less insulting variations of the term "queer." As Butler suggests, the reiteration of these shameful names constitutes performatively the identity of the queer subject. The act of naming makes Arjie aware of his difference from the expected norm and the resulting inevitable exclusion and loneliness. He observes: "I would be caught between the boys' and the girls' worlds, not belonging or wanted in either" (39). Yet, by challenging the authority of his grandmother, he rebels against the discourse of the family that wants to force him into a coercive gender role. Arjie's disturbing difference seems to justify the grandmother's severity; the boy's non-conforming conduct and his protest against the unfairness of the punishment make the penalty even more radical.

The mobility of gender is highlighted in *Funny Boy* by some marginal characters as well. Ironically, the captain of the competing team in the game of cricket is a girl—Meena—who wears dirty clothes and spits out guava seeds. Arjie's cousin Tanuja is a particularly big and assertive girl who plays with gender roles by disguising as the groom, and thus also turns the world of vestimentary codes upside down. Later in the novel, the protagonist's father encourages his son's friendship with Jegan, a muscular and particularly virile young man, for he believes that this epitome of manhood will help Arjie eradicate his queer tendencies. The narrator, however, presents Jegan's sexual orientation in an ambiguous light and it is in fact this model of masculinity that awakens the central protagonist's homoerotic desire. Thus, the novel emphasizes several times that the categories of gender are not clear and cannot be stabilized by the compulsory binary opposition.

Funny Boy highlights the performative aspect of gender through various other figures of theatrical disguise, mask, and transvestism. Arjie enjoys watching his mother dress for special occasions. The act of dressing acquires a ritualistic repetitive character and illustrates how gender unfolds through a series of performative operations. Considering the boy's interest unhealthy, Arjie's father forbids him to watch this masquerade of femininity. Yet, the protagonist continues to be attracted to the instruments of disguise which enable him to put into practice his fantasies of gender and to "assume" the mask of femininity. He deeply enjoys the transfiguration of self that occurs when Radha Aunty makes up his face and concludes: "You would have made a beautiful girl" (50). Hidden in his aunt's room, Arjie enacts the performance of womanliness playing with make-up and jewelry, painting his nails and admiring the effect of the transformation in the mirror. These examples of masquerade demonstrate the symbolic character of sexual identity.

However, growing up, the boy stops seeing the performance of womanhood as an innocent game. Radha Aunty's tragic love affair makes him aware of the political problems of Sri Lanka. The family's opposition to her relationship with Anil reveals to Arjie the hitherto unsuspected complexities of otherness. He realizes his family are Tamils, the oldest ethnic group of Sri Lanka, discriminated against by the dominating Sinhalese. His grandmother's father was killed by the Sinhalese in the riots of 1950s. Therefore, when the family learns that Radha is dating Anil, a Sinhalese, they force the young woman to leave Colombo in order to separate her from her lover. The family's condemnation intensifies Radha's feelings, yet, when she is attacked and severely beaten by the Sinhalese, she decides to marry the fiancé approved by the family. With dismay, Arjie comes to understand that love across race is not possible: the discourses of family and ethnicity coerce the individual into a submissive behavior.

During the ceremony of engagement, when Radha is transformed into a perfect bride owing to the magic power of dress and make-up, Arjie realizes that the elaborate performances that he has always dreamt of can, in fact, represent camouflage, dissimulation. As suggested by Riviere, in the act of masquerade a woman cannot mimic a genuine womanliness because such authentic femininity does not exist (Riviere 38). "The masquerade is a representation of femininity but then femininity is representation" (Heath 53). Thus, Arjie realizes the fragility of all identity construction and comes to see masquerade not as an innocent game but as an imposed mask. Similarly, in the next chapter, when his mother plays the perfect, beautiful hostess after her lover has been killed, Arjie notices the power of camouflage: "*Outwardly*, she seemed happy, almost gay"

(154; my emphasis). In the case of the female protagonists, masquerade comes to symbolize the subjection of the individual to the order of patriarchy. Arjie learns that it is constraint that sustains the performativity of gender. As Butler suggests, performativity is

> a regularized and constrained repetition of norms. And this repetition is not performed *by* a subject; this repetition is what enables a subject and constitutes the temporal condition for the subject. This iterability implies that "performance" is not a singular "act" or event, but a ritualized production, a ritual reiterated under and through constraint, under and through the force of prohibition and taboo, with the threat of ostracism and even death controlling and compelling the shape of the production, but not... determining it fully in advance. (Butler, *Gender* 95)

Arjie's mother relationship with Daryl Uncle illustrates the issue of marginalization in a more dramatic light. The love affair is contrasted with the patriarchal relation between Arjie's parents, regulated by the father's orders and prohibitions. The father remains an absent, remote figure who, however, blames the mother for the boy's queer deviations from the norm. During her husband's absence, Arjie's mother dares challenge the patriarchal order and get involved into an illicit love affair seeking for personal fulfillment. Moreover, Daryl Uncle, a reporter conducting investigations about the persecutions of the Tamils by the state, forces Arjie's mother to recognize the extent of the conflict between the Tamils and the Sinhalese. As a wealthy businessman's wife, she lives a secluded existence, unaware of the terrorist operations of the state. Only when her lover disappears does she become conscious of the mechanisms of the totalitarian regime. Faced with blackmail and social condemnation, Arjie's mother gives up her investigation and has to accept the fact of Daryl's death. The policeman in charge of the case threatens that he will reveal her secret relationship to her husband. Arjie himself accuses her of selfishness for having put the family in jeopardy. Thus, under the pressure of tradition and politics, Arjie's mother assumes her mask again, playing the role of the devoted wife when her husband returns from abroad.

The theme of masquerade as well as the social oppression of women that are illustrated by the subjection of Radha Aunty and Arjie's mother, further complicated by political discrimination, seem to suggest similarities between the social position of women and sexual minorities. The two last chapters of the novel illustrate Arjie's resistance to the coercive potential of the norm, his open rebellion towards injustice and oppression, and the ultimate failure of individual revolt against the macro-power's machinery of control.

When his father decides to send Arjie to The Queen Victoria Academy, he makes it clear that, as in the case of cricket, it is an attempt to traumatize his son into identification with masculinity. By announcing "The Academy will force you to become a man" (210), the father suggests his uneasiness concerning Arjie's subversive sexuality. Presented as a public school of the British type, the Victoria Academy appears an oppressive disciplinary institution. It exercises over its students what can be described in Foucauldian terms as "a constant pressure to conform to the same model. . . . So that they might all be like one another" (Foucault, *Discipline* 182). Arjie's first impressions at school highlight the brutality, aggression, and bravura that characterize the boys asserting their masculinity. Warning him against the sadistic principal of the school, Diggy emphasizes that he must never complain to the parents: "Once you come to The Queen Victoria Academy you are a man. Either you take it like a man or the other boys will look down on you" (211). Thus, masculinity is defined negatively, through the rejection and disparagement of the feminine:

> Compulsive masculinity is about the pursuit of self-esteem; the desire to regress, to experience "feminine" emotions, constitutes a built-in internal threat to boys' and men's self-esteem. Certain basic human emotions—especially grief and fear—are experienced as internal threats to self-esteem by boys seeking separation from their mothers. (Beneke 69)

Furthermore, in the seemingly asexual context of the public school, femininity seems to represent threatening otherness, "defined by its pronounced sexuality: not by some more or less clear sexual identity, but just the presence of a sexual element in the Other's nature" (Glasenapp 136). Because of his visible alterity, Arjie seems to represent the figure of the other *par excellence*, the scapegoat over whom the other boys have to prove their manhood. His position of a victim is rendered more acute when he finds himself in a Sinhalese class. For compulsive masculinities "function by asserting their superiority over the 'other,' whether that be gay men, younger men, women, or subordinated ethnic groups" (Roper and Tosh, quoted in Glasenapp 136).

The atmosphere of victimization is dissipated by the interference of Shehan Soyza, who derives his power from his sexual relations with the head prefect of the school. The figure of Shehan puts into question the easy binarism of the construction of masculinity. The narrator's descriptions emphasize his beauty, fragility, and sensuality. Arjie experiences an immediate attraction to Shehan and their erotic relationship helps him finally comprehend the significance of the otherness attributed to him since the bride-bride incident: "The difference within me that I sometimes felt I had, that had brought me so much confusion, whatever this difference, it was shared by Shehan" (256). Hoping that this difference will crystalize itself, Arjie gets involved in a friendship with Shehan despite the homophobic warnings of his brother Diggy. However, the first sexual act between the two boys inspires Arjie with a feeling of guilt, revulsion and shame that cause him to reject Shehan violently. At this point Arjie seems to have internalized the prohibitions of the patriarchal family aiming to protect the heterosexual norm. He believes that he has committed a terrible crime and is ready to beg for absolution. Soon, however, he liberates himself from fear and the internalized discourse of repression and accepts his feeling of love for Shehan.

In order to win his lover back, Arjie is ready to challenge the ultimate authority of the disciplinary institution, the principal of the school, Black Tie. A Tamil brought up under the colonial regime, the latter believes in the power of what Foucault would call the "disciplinary gaze" (Foucault, *Discipline* 174), the meticulous regulations, constant surveillance and control. During one of his fussy inspections he notices that Shehan wears his hair long, which constitutes a direct challenge to the school's code of conduct. From then on Black Tie exercises over Shehan a series of sadistic punishments, which seem to have a symbolic function since Shehan represents the ultimate non-observance, the extreme "abnormal" that must be broken down and normalized. Moreover, Black Tie decides to use Arjie in his power-struggle with the vice-president of the school, a Sinhalese. At the prize-giving ceremony Arjie is supposed to recite two colonial poems celebrating the glory of the school. Thus, the principal hopes to win the sympathy of the guest of honor, a minister of cabinet. Traumatized by the sight of Black Tie's cane, Arjie is unable to recite the poems during rehearsals and, subsequently, he undergoes severe physical punishment. Shehan, whom Black Tie orders to assist Arjie in studying the poems, is punished together with his friend. Eventually, Black Tie disposes of the cane and Arjie manages to recite the poems in his presence, nevertheless, the principal continues to punish Shehan. It is then that Arjie experiences a strong feeling of rebellion against the absurd code of the disciplinary institution. In a revealing passage, he connects these acts of injustice with the preceding examples of oppression, and revolts against the power of the norm:

> Right and wrong, fair and unfair had nothing to do with how things really were. I thought of Shehan and myself. What had happened between us in the garage was not wrong. For how could loving Shehan be bad? Yet, if my parents or anybody else discovered this love, I would be in terrible trouble. . . . How was it that some people got to decide what was correct or not, just or unjust? It had to do with who was in charge; everything had to do with who held power and who didn't. If you were powerful like Black Tie or my father you got to decide what was right or wrong. If you were like Shehan or me you had no choice but to follow what they said. (273-4)

Arjie's final act of defiance, his deliberate confusion of the words of the poems which ridicules the principal's subsequent speech, can be therefore seen as an ultimate rebellion against the mechanisms of power. Pretending to conform to the "disciplinary gaze," Arjie manages, however, to assert an independent subject-position. This form of agency constitutes an example of Foucault's "technologies of the self"; although the individual is still situated within the discourse of power, s/he is able to use and abuse it and to show resistance to it (see Foucault *Technologies of the Self*). It is important that Arjie's love for Shehan takes precedence over ethnic loyalty: his subversive act brings about the downfall of the Tamil principal. The need to protest against homophobia and the marginalizing procedures of the micro-powers proves stronger than his attachment to the family and the ethnic group. The incident also illustrates how Arjie gains independence from the family and drifts towards identification with Shehan, based on the acceptance of his sexual orientation. This newly discovered sense of community seems to suggest some sources of power outside of the norms established by the society:

> As I gazed at Amma [the mother], I felt a sudden sadness. What had happened between Shehan and me over the last few days had changed my relationship with her forever. I was no longer part of my family in the same way. I now inhabited a world they didn't understand and into which they couldn't follow me.
> Shehan was standing by the classroom door, waiting for me. . . we began to walk together towards the stairs that led down to the auditorium. (284-5)

Nevertheless, the epilogue of the novel presented in the form of a journal describing the riots in Sri Lanka between July and August 1983 shows the individual as powerless in front of the macro-power of the state. The persecutions of the Tamils, the looting of Tamil shops, the cover-up of the media, and the open hostility towards the Tamils conveyed in the Sinhalese President's official broadcast make the tension grow. Arjie's family realize their vulnerability when they are forced to escape from their house which is destroyed by the mob and when, eventually, Arjie's grandparents are burnt alive by the crowd in their car. Together with his relatives, Arjie comes to understand that the mechanisms of power have excluded them from the homogeneous construction of nation: "I long to be out of this country. I don't feel at home in Sri Lanka any longer, will never feel safe again" (304). The only solution seems emigration to Canada, a frightening prospect, as, due to the Sri Lankan government's financial regulations, they will have to accept the plight of destitute refugees. Arjie's parting with Shehan after a seven-month relationship is presented in dramatic terms. However, the ethnic difference (Shehan is not Tamil) introduces distance between the lovers: "This awareness did not change my feelings for him, it was simply there, like a thin translucent screen through which I watched him" (302). Thus, the political machinery separates them forever.

Focusing on the mechanisms of power and exclusion, Shyam Selavadurai's *Funny Boy* illustrates the interconnection of micro-powers and macro-power in their attempts to differentiate, homogenize and normalize so as to protect the interests of the dominant groups. While the novel highlights the individual's vulnerability in a totalitarian regime, it also illustrates ambivalent strategies of resistance against the norm as imposed by the discourses of family and heterosexuality. By presenting various forms of oppression and opposition to it, Selvadurai draws our attention to the similar position of women and gay men in the patriarchal society. However, if the female characters are completely subjected to the male order and the performative ritual of fixed gender identification, Arjie dares rebel against the homophobic, marginalizing mechanisms of patriarchy. By means of cross-dressing and masquerade, he evades the power of compulsive masculinity, highlighting the mobile character of gender. Finally, pretending to conform to the norms imposed by the "disciplinary gaze," the protagonist works out some form of agency. His opposition can be interpreted as a symbolical act of protest against any form of oppression, the marginalization of sexual otherness but also other forms of alterity. *Funny Boy* makes us thus reconsider the issue of resistance, suggesting that it is not simply a transparent reversal of power, but a more complex strategy through which subject-positions are inhabited by individuals *within* the discourses of subjection. Selvadurai seems to support Foucault's assertion that "nothing in society will be changed if the mechanisms of power that function outside, below and alongside the State apparatuses, on a much more minute and everyday level, are not also changed" (Foucault, *Power* 60). The struggle against the marginalization of othernesss and the "normalizing" mechanisms of power as depicted in the novel show that power relations must be undermined from within, thus allowing certain forms of agency and individuality.

Works Cited

Beneke, Timothy. *Proving Manhood: Reflections on Men and Sexism.* Berkeley: University of California Press, 1997.

Butler, Judith. "Critically Queer." *Bodies That Matter. On the Discursive Limits of "Sex."* New York: Routledge, 1993. Polish version: "Krytycznie Queer." Trans. A. Rzepa. *Furia Pierwsza* 7.1 (December 2000): 37-58.

———. Gender Trouble: Feminism and the Subversion of Identity. New York and London: Routledge, 1999.

Foucault, Michel. *Discipline and Punish.* Trans. A. Sheridan. London: Penguin Books, 1991.

———. *Technologies of the Self: A Seminar with Michel Foucault.* Eds. L.Martin et al. Amherst: University of Massachussetts Press, 1988.

———. *Power / Knowledge*. Ed. C. Gordon. Trans. C. Gordon et al. New York: Pantheon Books, 1980.

Glasenapp, Małgorzata. "*Femina Non Grata*: Femininity in Exile in British Boys' School Stories." *The Writing of Exile*. Eds. W. Kalaga and T. Rachwał. Katowice: Wydawnictwo Naukowe "Śląsk," 2001. 127-138.

Heath, Stephen. "Joan Riviere and the Masquerade." *Formations of Fantasy*. Eds. V. Burgin et al. London and New York: Routledge, 1987. 45-61.

Riviere, Joan. "Womanliness as a Masquerade." *Formations of Fantasy*. Eds. V. Burgin et al. London and New York: Routledge, 1987. 35-44.

Selvadurai, Shyam. *Funny Boy*. Toronto: McClelland and Stewart, 1994.

"INTO ANOTHER WOMAN:" WRITING THE HOMOEROTIC IN VERNON LEE'S *LADY TAL*

EWA MACURA

> The sight or the idea of a person of her own sex has no power to excite [woman's] sex centre to any form of activity, and hence man must be her ideal of beauty.
>
> Max Nordau, Degeneration

Lady Tal, Vernon Lee's heroine, whose homophonic name anticipates an excess of sorts, is from the beginning gossiped into a "strange creature" (200) and "a riddle" (206), suspended in speculations which rehearse her enigmatic character but do not secure any solution. The story never takes her viewpoint (except in dialogues) and her peculiar biography though revealed early in the text, fails to account for her strangeness. Both these epithets, contained by her nickname, blend curiously her somewhat disproportionate appearance *and* behaviour, transposing cause and effect in order to design "physical deviations as simultaneously the source and the marker of mental and moral inferiority" (Hamilton 62). Thus in accord with late nineteenth-century fantasies of bodies gone wrong, the emphasis on the visibility of a certain disproportion, where an exterior excess translates into an interior one, and vice versa, works to foreground Lady Tal's irregularity. Yet clearly this irregularity does not follow simply from an inside/outside translation but rather form the fact that hers is a woman's body. It is because she is a gendered creature that both her body *and* actions can be read as excessive and that their encoding is possible at all. Measured against the parameters that delineate the properly feminine she proves unable to meet gender demands as her body fails to inhabit the right proportions. Lady Tal, as "a six foot high," (206) "terrible aristocratic giantess" (226) surpasses the limits refusing transparency and resisting intelligibility.

If Lady Tal's overshaped body implicates her in a vexing strangeness, one that seems to delay straightforward associations, then her aristocratic pedigree hints at a set of more accessible references. Morally corrupt by definition, aristocracy was a token of mental and physical deterioration that could accommodate a wide range of deviations (see for example Hamilton). Lady Tal clearly diverges from bourgeois scenarios of happiness, marriage in particular. Conjuring up a dreary vision of marital life and a humdrum wifely existence, she asks: "Wouldn't living with the Bishop of Torcello, in that musty little house with all the lichen stains and mosquito nests, and nothing but Attila's throne to call upon—be fun compared with that?" (245). Marriage is definitely no fun and this is why it cannot bring diversion into her otherwise uninteresting life: "I am bored with all life. . . ; but to marry this particular Clarence, or any other Clarence that may be disporting himself about, wouldn't somehow diminish the boringness of things" (246). The problem is that Lady Tal feels excruciatingly bored. With lots of time and loads of money to spare she wastes both. The abuse comes not with a failure to spend but with a failure to spend appropriately. More grossly, however, neither the money nor the time are properly hers. Having inherited both from her husband, and her singleness long overdue now, she lives on borrowed time. If boredom signifies dissipation it also presumes lassitude. Even when she ponders on the possibility of having the dullness diminished she not only foregoes any effort, but also makes it redundant altogether: "What do you think *one* might *do* to *make* things a little less dull? But perhaps everything is equally dull" (248, emphasis mine). Weary enough, Lady Tal rejects the blessings of exertion placing herself beyond doing and making and thus beyond the ethos of work and its economy where you have to work your way to pleasure. Boredom becomes non-production, (which is not the same as to say that boredom results from lack of any productive activity), an effortless and wasteful consumption, not only because Lady Tal does not do anything but also because boredom (and therefore consumption) fails to produce pleasure.

If anything can relieve Lady Tal's boredom, it is *Christina*, whom she singles out as the only worthwhile pursuit: "On the whole, my one interest in life is evidently destined to be *Christina*" (250). The singularity of this interest reveals also a singularity of the attachment. One to a woman and the only one Lady Tal forms and avows, it stands out in her biography credited with "an extraordinary absence of human emotion" (233). *Christina,* moreover, both is and designates an outside, for if all is dull "except dear old *Christina*" (248) as Lady Tal remarks, then she oversteps that everything delineating its limits. As an exception she is also beyond the economy that governs the space of boredom. Yet the outside to which she belongs is not a space where consumption and non-production are simply substituted for their opposites. If *Christina* is not subject to consumption it does not mean that she remains untouched. Indeed, *Christina* needs more than a few touches and it is touching that narrates their relationship in most palpable terms, becoming the locus of erotics and potential pleasure. Yet the touches have to be ruinous if *Christina* is to be touched at all. This strange condition of their encounter knots production and non-production for if Lady Tal is for once exerting an effort then it goes into undoing rather than doing. Liable to ravages of Lady Tal's busy hands *Christina* is touched into existence and only thus can emerge as her lover. And yet the ruin inflicted upon *Christina's* body parallels her ruination within the story. Expectedly enough, *Christina* does not exist, not because *Christina* is a novel that Lady Tal is writing, and the heroine of this novel, but more importantly, because the novel itself is impossible.

We learn about this impossibility from Jervase Marion, Lady Tal's literary advisor. Marion is an American novelist, apparently of recognised standing, and undeniably endowed with remarkable psychological insight. Somehow against his will and "in a wholly unintelligible way" (209), he finds himself burdened with an unpleasant duty to read Lady Tal's "first attempt at a novel" (207). When after a string of complaints Marion finally and reluctantly sets about reading, he, much to the reader's disappointment, offers only flippant and evasive remarks. Little of the story is revealed (one paragraph only is quoted) and Marion's major objections are to Lady Tal's ignorance of punctuation and to her unintelligible style. Because "her sentences invariably consisted either of three words, or of twenty-seven lines, and her grammar and spelling were nowhere" (213), Marion plans to offer her "Blair's Rhetoric" and "Stops: and how to manage them" and thus quench Lady Tal's literary zeal. Yet Marion's resolutions come to nothing for Lady Tal refuses "to be put off with mere remarks about grammar and stops" (216) and demands some more useful criticism. Marion does not beat about the bushes, and with an air of superiority, bluntly tells her: "your novel, if you will allow me to say a rude thing, is utterly impossible" (217).

What follows is Marion's rather impatient explanations which again thwart the reader's expectations for his attacks are directed not to what Lady Tal writes but what she doesn't write. She is, we are told, "perpetually taking all sorts of knowledge for granted," her "characters do not sufficiently explain themselves," (217) and she does not quite understand what she is writing. While Marion scolds Lady Tal's insufficient language, her irritating habit of leaving things unsaid, the outrage intimated in his "utterly impossible" addresses the bare fact that there*is* something unsaid in the first place.[1] Evidently, Marion reads Lady Tal's practice of avoidance as indicative of a wilful concealment. His response of a flat denial then has also to do with becoming privy to some ugly secret he will now feel obliged to safeguard. The fact is that throughout the story, the content of the novel as well as what it fails to say, will remain obscure. If in Lee's text the unspoken is to convey the impossible then it is Marion's refusal to relate her narrative, more than Lady Tal's reticence, that registers the intensity of the unspeakable. Consequently, Marion will never speak of the details of their "lively interchange of communication" (219) which they establish with an aim of recasting Lady Tal's manuscript, nor of the nature of his "perpetual criticisms" and her endless "corrections" (219). Marion must obviously insist on saying nothing of what is and how it is altered lest the secret be disclosed. Yet his silence might also indicate that there is no more secret to keep, for to recast the novel is to cast it in the "speakable," to say it anew and say all. Lady Tal, Marion tells us, must learn "to cultivate a . . . lucid style" (212), lucidity becoming a promise not only of intelligibility but as well of sanity and thus normalcy. Indeed, to correct the novel is to set it right, not to say straight, to restore an order both masculine and heteronormative, the manifestation of which, on a most superficial level, is proper grammar and punctuation; an order which brings under control the leaky and unruly text and leaves no room for dark secrets. And yet to sanitise *Christina* is at the same time to sanitise Lady Tal who "[carried] through life a rather exotic little romance which no one must suspect" (241). When Marion declares that *Christina* "was evidently the real Lady Tal" (251), he conflates both women as he assumes a mimetic relationship between the text and its author, thus turning them into the sharers of the same secret.

It would seem therefore that it is this "lively interchange" between Marion and Lady Tal that is given focus in the story. He arrives in Venice in order "to give himself a complete holiday" (195) and drop, for a while, the habit of studying people yet he ends up being instantly attracted to Lady Tal's enigmatic character. Cast in the mode of endless speculations and ruminations it is Marion's fascination with Lady Tal that impels the storyline. Undeniably, this fascination owes a little to all the unflattering gossip which introduces Lady Tal into the narrative space. What captures Marion's attention, however, is her abnormally outgrown body. "Very tall, straight, and strongly built," "stalwart," and of "great strength, size" (198), "with a huge strongly-knit frame" (210), "too strong, too large" (214), this body will come to threaten the boundaries of both gender and sexuality. Aesthetically speaking, it does not befit a woman; more grossly, however, it unmans Marion, casting him into a weaker, feminine position. What is more, it fails to yield what its anatomy, however unshapely, should promise. That is, while her body is overabundant, her femininity rather deficient. Marion does not find her "an appealing woman" (210) at all, and what exacerbates his dislike is Lady Tal's overly masculine demeanour. She bullies men verbally, owns "a masculine voice with the falsetto tone," executes "angular movements," enjoys "brusque, bantering speech," dismayingly, is "able to take care of herself" (210), and wears "mannish flannel garments" (231). It will not be far-fetched to suggest that such misalignment, in the *fin de siècle* context, would make Lady Tal's sexuality highly suspect. Indeed, theorised by late Victorian sexologists (for example Edward Carpenter), it was indicative of sexual inversion, a then scientific term for homosexuality. Aware of Lady Tal's intermediate position Marion subjects her to a meticulous psychological scrutiny which is to reveal her soul and thus ease his homophobic fear. The problem is that Lady Tal hasn't got a soul, and Marion clearly links its absence with her appalling masculinity. When he first ventures into her portrayal, he concludes that it was "the want of soul which constituted the strength of Lady Tal" (210). The soul Lady Tal so obviously lacks, in Marion's view, is a feminine one. Throughout the story Marion will struggle in search of her soul, one that would properly match her body, in order to overcome the "vague repulsion" he feels "due to her dreadful strength" (210). And again, Marion proves a knowledgeable psychologist and sexologist. In Edward Carpenter's words, the misalignment typical of sexual inversion was, more precisely, characterised as a "crosswise connexion between "soul" and "body" (Carpenter). When Marion repeatedly remarks that Lady Tal has no soul (213, 230, 231, 239) he clearly bemoans its misplacement. But, Marion understands, what is misplaced can just as well be replaced. Wondering "in what portion of [her] person that soul could possibly be located" he does not ask about its location but rather reckons the possibility itself of having the soul reinstated to where it naturally belongs. Marion and Lady Tal's lively interchange of communication becomes then a therapeutic session where secrets must be abandoned and souls returned to their bodies.

What Marion fails to notice, however, is that his therapeutic endeavours bring Lady Tal and *Christina* into a rather intimate contact. Throughout the story, *Christina* moves between reality and fiction, Marion being partly and unwittingly responsible for this movement when he, in his imagination, lets her merge with Lady Tal, and thus emerge as a potential lover. She is also animated by her name through its figuration within the narrative, a name that always promises a real woman as its referent even as it continues to withdraw that promise to offer a text instead. This abiding anticipation, produced by the name's failure to yield an unambiguous translation, will come to a momentary suspension from Lady Tal when, relating the exertions of the previous night, she not only dissociates *Christina* from the realm of fiction but also describes what cannot but be their love encounter: "That novel is turning me into another woman: the power of sinning, as the Salvationists say, has been extracted out of my nature even by the rootlets; I sat up till two last night after returning from the Lido, and got up this morning at six, all for the love of *Christina* and literature" (225). Perhaps the passage does not easily translate into a homoerotic scenario. Couched in a language of heterosexual imperative with its prescriptions for a single woman, it reclaims Lady Tal as a marriageable widow, chastity incarnate, who successfully sublimates her power of sinning into a time-consuming occupation; one that keeps her too busy and too exhausted for any kind of mind or bodily transgressions. Yet if we transpose the causes and effects which structure the passage, this welcome transformation might just as well be taking a different direction. If rewriting proves so exhausting it is because, after all, it does require a dose of physical labour. It is about handling, holding, thumbing, fingering, feeling, above all about touching, both the text's and the woman's body. If this tangible proximity is to carry a highly erotic charge then the exhaustion suggested as a kind of inaugural gesture that forecloses heterosexual intrigue in order to maintain moral order, becomes, in fact, an end, both an aim and a climactic completion, resonating with a pleasurable fatigue. To go along this line of interpretation requires a broader notion of sexuality and desire, one that would accommodate a wider range of erotic experiences. In her essay "Refiguring Lesbian Desire," Elizabeth Grosz takes desire beyond its most privileged site, that is genitality, offering a framework in which sexual relations not only partake of other relations like those for instance "of the writer to pen and paper" (181) but also inscribe desire at the "interfaces between one part and another of bodies or body-things, ". . . between a hand and a breast, a tongue and a cunt, a mouth and food, a nose and a rose" (182). Thus desire materialises in an encounter between surfaces, indeed, as Grosz argues, it inscribes them as surfaces which become erotogenic zones always provisional and ephemeral. Importantly then, no surface is ever predetermined as erotic; ready and able to invest desire because "any thing can form part of its circuit, can be absorbed into its operations" (183).

Vernon Lee's story might be read as a tale of censorship, with Marion's policing intervention which aims to restore *Christina* (and Lady Tal as well) within the "speakable," the intelligible, and thus acceptable. Yet if rewriting becomes an erotic gesture in its inscription of desire upon surfaces, upon bodies and body-things, then it is only through this intervention that it can operate at all. Since the story narrates the love encounter between women within the prohibition, the impossibility with which Marion introduces the novel not only immunises that which emerges out as possibility but becomes as well its enabling condition.

Notes

1. See Neill Matheson for his discussion of Wilde's trial (1895) and the panic it caused in relation to "evasiveness as the sign of concealed transgression." ("Talking Horrors: James, Euphemism, and the Spectre of Wilde"). Although Lee's story was written before the infamous trials, evasiveness seems to function here in the same way.

Works Cited

Carpenter, Edward. *The Intermediate Sex: A Study of Some Transitional Types of Men and Women*. 16 Aug. 2003. <http://www.fordham.edu/halsall/pwh/carpenter-is.html>.

Grosz, Elizabeth. "Refiguring Lesbian Desire." *Space, Time, and Perversion*. New York: Routledge, 1995. 173-185.

Hamilton, Lisa K. "New Women and 'Old' Men: Gendering Degeneration." *Women and British Aestheticism*. Ed. Talia Schaffer and Kathy Alexis Psomiades. Charlottesville & London: University Press of Virginia, 1999.

Lee, Vernon. "Lady Tal." *Daughters of Decadence: Women Writers of the Fin-de-Siècle*. Ed. Elaine Showalter. London: Virago Press, 2000. 192-261

Matheson, Neill. "Talking Horrors: James, Euphemism, and the Spectre of Wilde." *American Literature* 71.4 (1999): 709-750.

CRISIS HOUSE: METAPHORS OF QUEER DEPRESSION

ZUZANNA SZATANIK

> To name ourselves rather than be named we must first see ourselves. For some of us this will not be easy. So long unmirrored, we may have forgotten how we look. Nevertheless, we can't theorize in a void; we must have evidence.
>
> (O'Grady)

> . . . thanks to the house, a great many of our memories are housed, and if the house is a bit elaborate, if it has a cellar and a garret, nooks and corridors, our memories have refuges that are all the more clearly delineated. All our lives we come back to them in our daydreams. A psychoanalyst should, therefore, turn his attention to this simple localization of our memories. I should like to give the name of topoanalysis to this auxiliary of psychoanalysis. Topoanalysis, then, would be the systematic psychological study of the sites of our intimate lives.
>
> (Bachelard)

Memory and daydreaming, literature and *topoi*, poetry and intimacy—all these concepts, intricately interwoven, underly Bachelardian analytical thinking about literature. Enjoying the status of a "stately" classic, the theoretical proposition that Bachelard offered the world resurfaces today in a poststructural version of the criticism of consciousness, which approach—aware of the intellectual developments of the recent decades—legitimizes its precursor's intuitions anew. The present paper is an exercise in such a "thematic" study of literature, or, in other words, is an attempt to offer a perspective which could encompass phenomena usually addressed separately and studied by means of seemingly incompatible methodological tools. The object of my study is thus to map the imaginative relationships obtaining between space, gendered identity, and natural landscape informing the poetry of one of the more intriguing Canadian poets, Chandra Mayor.

Topography, topoi, topoanalysis

In Bachelard's phrasing, "[one's] unconscious is housed" (*The Poetics of Space* 10). The architecture and unique interior design of such a "mental abode" is the result of a particular arrangement of a "body of images" (*The Poetics of Space* 16) which, organized according to the rules of complex, immanent poetics, determine a "topography of an intimate being" (*The Poetics of Space* 16). And yet the house of my particular interest is not "homy"; it is Chandra Mayor's "Crisis House"—an intermediary space between the "normal" and the "abnormal," and a reverie Bachelard would probably see as therapeutic:

> . . . we shall have to introduce a slight nuance at the very base of topoanalysis. [writes Bachelard—comment Z.S.]. I pointed out earlier that the unconscious is housed. It should be added that is well and happily housed, in the space of its happiness. The normal unconscious knows how to make itself at home everywhere, and psychoanalysis comes to the assistance of the ousted unconscious, of the unconscious that has been roughly and insidiously dislodged. But psychoanalysis sets the human being in motion, rather then at rest. It calls on him to live outside the abodes of his unconscious, to enter into life's adventures, to come out of himself. And naturally, its action is a salutary one. Because we must also give an exterior destiny to the interior being. To accompany psychoanalysis in this salutary action, we should have to undertake a topoanalysis of all the space that has invited us to come out of ourselves. (*The Poetics of Space* 10-11)

The "Crisis House" may be a salutary measure, but nonetheless one needs to bear in mind that the crisis house in itself is a place where one goes when one is not crazy enough to go to an institution, but no longer fit to be called "normal." It is a queer place; and in Chandra Mayor's poem it is *queer* in more than solely the colloquial sense of the word.

In the poem titled "Continue" and in series of five "sub-poems" under an umbrella title of the "Crisis House," the lyrical I of Mayor's—herself a homoerotic poet—is neither heterosexual, nor lesbian, and—to make things even more complex—probably Canadian. Moreover, the unattainability of any self-identification (including sexual self-definition) appears to be one of the major reasons of identity crisis the poet addresses. And thus, if Bachelard is right to say that one's unconscious "is housed," then the poetic space of Mayor's reverie of the past—the house described in her poem "Continue"—may be read as corresponding to the mental "organisation" of a mind in crisis. Creative writing, after all, is always "tinged" with existence: "[There is a] radical difference," writes Bachelard,

> between the nocturnal dream (*rêve*) and reverie, the radical difference, a difference deriving form phenomenology; while the dreamer of the nocturnal dream is a shadow who has lost his self (*moi*), the dreamer of reverie, if he is a bit philosophical, can formulate a *cogito* at the center of his dreaming self (*son moi rêveur*). Put another way, *reverie is oneiric activity in which a glimmer of consciousness subsists* [italics—Z.S.]. The dreamer of reverie is present in his reverie. Even when the reverie gives the impression of the flight out of the real, out of time and place, the dreamer of reverie knows that it is he who is absenting himself—he, in flesh and blood, who is becoming a "spirit," a phantom of the past or of voyage. (*The Poetics of Reverie* 150)

The dreamer-poet, phantom of her own past, offers herself a reverie of a house that is never a real shelter, a house that no longer is a frigate capable of withstanding the force of "the surrounding storm."[1] Permeable, leaking and transforming, the house in "Continue" lets the tempestuous outside in; the entropy of the unruly, liquid exterior informs it.

The Flooded House

In the poem, the homely space of a safe ship becomes an interior of a sunken wreck. The structure, once familiar, becomes a part of the impenetrable landscape of the bottom of the sea; water invades it benumbing the lonely sailor. Or, still more adequately—the house, located perhaps too close to the shore, but once believed to be solid, is eventually flooded by some overwhelming *tsunami*:

> Morning rolls onto your chest and you wake gasping
> For breath and reason. Your mouth is dry and sour
> and you gulp down guilt, ignore the heaps of clothes
> and newspapers and shoes in every
> corner. You have to get up. The floor is gritty as sand

beneath your bare feet and your head is heavy
on your shoulders. You are walking through water.
If you open your mouth you'll drown. The cat weaves
Through your legs creating whirlpools around your ankles.
There was somewhere you meant to go, you began
with determination and a destination but you find
yourself hooked through your lip and you can't
remember the reason for the struggle. The sun
is excruciatingly slow as it spins across the sky.
Your house is filled with wreckage and debris
and your thoughts are barely glimpsed
through silty water. Your heart hammers
fists under your ribs, but the way to continue
living is to stand very still. The way to continue
breathing is not to scream. The way to continue
fighting is to acquiesce to meaninglessness,
aimlessness, and terror. You find yourself a way. ("Continue" 26)

"I know my ways, you find yourself a way." Indeed, a position expectedly taken by one whose house has been shaken to its foundations by an overpowering force. Yet, as a sympathetic "construction inspector," the critic probably ought to give some lee to the shaken lyrical I, sunken in depression and striving to survive by concentrating all remaining energies on sole surviving. The inspector is not a doctor, s/he is expected to build a hypothesis of why the house sank. Why, let me.

Foundations

The examination of the locale starts with the scrutiny of the murky ground the house has been built on. The house, whose present condition may be expected to have partly depended on the location and solidity of its foundations, originally rose in a space it eventually came to enclose within. Importantly, this space itself is a "gray, protoplasmic fuzz outside [the American] borders" (Atwood 171)— the snow-bound Canada suffering from the borderline non-definability. According to Katherine Monk it is "emptiness—or negative space—[that] becomes a defining principle in the Canadian psyche, Canadian art and Canadian film" (89). The idea of Canada as emptiness finds it metaphorical illustration in a striking comparison: Monk defines Canada resorting to the *lack of defining categories* and likens the country to a doughnut. As much as the doughnut would not be a doughnut if it did not have a hole in the middle, Canada gains its identity owing to the lack of definition. Monk aptly claims that "the hole may be nothing, but without it, a doughnut is just a pastry" (89). Perhaps this is the reason why Canada (to borrow Evelynn Hammond's metaphor), like a black hole, can be detected "by its effects on the region of space where it is located" (149). Perhaps this is also the reason why Canadians, when presented in works of Canadian writing, whose aim was to grasp the elusive nature of the Canadian identity, "are defined by what [they] are not, more so than what [they] are" (Monk 89).

The Canadians inhabit the landscape that is stereotypically conceived of as a "snow-bound void," and they melt away in the blazing light of their powerful neighbor. They are *almost* Americans, but not *quite* so. In the Internet-distributed satirical "Map of the World According to America," Canada is the land of "our friendly, but backwards neighbors":

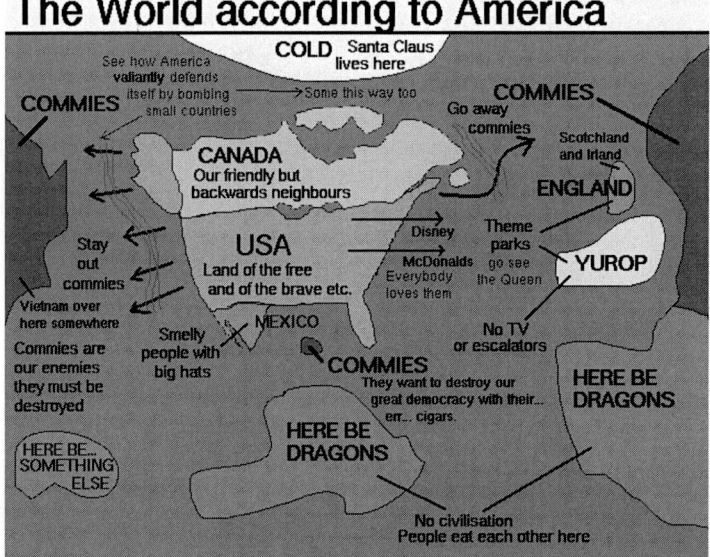

The South Park characters "blame" the easy scapegoat, "Canada," for all the evil of the world, and the Monty Python pokes fun at the cross-dressing, oxy*moronic*, Canadian lumberjack, "who's OK." Owing to its "blurredness," Canada must be tamed: if beyond comprehension in familiar categories, it must be either ridiculed, or patronized. Indeed, plastic, Canada must be molded into whatever shape to be grasped.

In Canadian texts addressing the issue of the essence of "Canadianness," the self-reflexive knowledge of the surrounding emptiness informing their rhetoric, as well as the awareness of the Self being (read as) the Other permeating their metaphorics, provide the creative urge for the speaking Is to call into existence what is not so much a "Canadian self-definition" as "Canadian self-undefinability." Canadianness is defined by the absence, and it is in the Canadian ground that Chandra Mayor's flooded house had its foundations.

Holes in the Superstructure

With the foundations set in w hole, the superstructure of the poetic matter—the intricately woven fabric of imagination—may be doubted to be wholesome. Moreover, the poetics of the reverie, being the principle of the architecture of the house, reveals traits of liquidity. Instead of right angles, hard-edged bricks, and straight lines, the house in a somewhat effeminate fashion, features soft matter. It is built of consciousness that is not definite enough to keep entropy at bay. It is built of the consciousness that grows around double nothingness founded on a hole.

Hamlet. Ophelia. N(O)thing.

The cascading metaphor above is not a new one; its well known Shakespearian use illustrates it best:

HAMLET
Lady, shall I lie in your lap?

(Lying down at OPHELIA's feet)
OPHELIA
No, my lord.

HAMLET
I mean, my head upon your lap?

OPHELIA
Ay, my lord.

HAMLET
Do you think I meant country matters?

OPHELIA
I think nothing, my lord.

HAMLET
That's a fair thought to lie between maids' legs.

OPHELIA
What is, my lord?

HAMLET
Nothing.

OPHELIA
You are merry, my lord.

HAMLET
Who, I?

OPHELIA
Ay, my lord.

The "fair," thought to lie in between maid's legs, is the promise of a *fiesta*, the promise of sex, the promise of the vagina, which, in Shakespeare's time was already euphemized as either "o" or "nothing," and which for good ol' Freud was the defining feature of femininity. Such is the dominant discourse of the phallogocentric culture; for centuries the lack of penis *was supposed* to be the source of envy, and femininity itself came to believe that its self-definition must be based on the "prominent lack." The feminine body of images, of which Mayor's house consists is manufactured by a self defined through n(o)thing.

In the poem titled "This Little Girl," Mayor writes:

> This little girl grows up around the hole in her belly. She fills it with
> shiny bits of flattery, the glint of sunlight on hubcaps, the interminable
> ticking of clocks, and cigarettes that smolder forever. (24)

Clearly, "This Little Girl" develops around the emptiness. She defines herself through absence, "lack, incompleteness, deficiency, envy with respect to the only sexuality in which value resides" (Felman 119), as "identity [is] conceived as a solely masculine sameness, apprehended as male self-presence, and consciousness-to-itself" (119). The dominant symbolic order of phallogocentrism renders the discourse of femininity as "minus-discourse," the feminine identity is present owing to absence. Defined by lack, it DOES exist, ephemerically. The House is endangered: its foundations suspended in a hole, its walls, nooks and corridors of ephemeric matter which grew around a hole, and—as is easy to show—its roof mighty leaky, too—the house could not conceivably be any more "Crisis" than it is.

And—on top of that...

—a hole, of course. Or, more precisely, a hole beyond the symbolic order, and thus not even a hole. The emptiness in the little girl's belly may be discussed as standing in opposition to solid, prominently present matter to be found in the analogous location in her male counterparts, but what tops off Chandra Mayor's speaking I's reverie—resists discourse, it cannot even be identified as nothing, it is always neither, it is a non-identity, it is *queer*.

The "phantom" of Mayor's past, the female character of her poems is "unsymbolised"—both to herself and the external world. The house presented in the poem "Continue" cannot be defined as the inside, nor can it be defined as the outside, and thus is a structure beyond comprehension, beyond the symbolic order. The foundations of this house rest upon nothing, the walls, defined by lack, do not "guarantee a separation between an inner and an outer world" (Pouchard 53) and thus the whole "domestic" structure merges with the landscape eventually becoming the landscape: the house is flooded, there is sand on the floor; heaps of clothes, "wreckage and debris" form the messy, contradictory scenery that is neither "natural," nor "artificial."

As the house in the poem *is* a poetic analogue of a reverie rooted in the consciousness of a Canadian (who *is defined by what s/he is not*), uses as its construction material the rhetoric daydreamt by a woman (who *is defined by what she is not*), and *queer* sexuality (that *is defined by what it is not*), the house *is* the non-house.

Instead of "[strengthening] the happiness of inhabiting" by means of contrast, landscape transforms the seemingly familiar sphere into an oxymoronic space, into the interior which is nether the shelter, nor the wilderness, neither tame, nor wild, neither the Self, nor the Other.

The landscape that invades the house is hostile: it makes it difficult to walk, to talk, and even to breathe. The outside which moves inside, transforms the house into empty, unsymbolised space. Such a space, less clearly defined than the a hole in a doughnut, or the hole in the little girl's belly, in Mayor's poem becomes the hole into which her speaking I plunges only to come round, like "Alice in Distressland" (Kristeva 74) in a reality distorted by the *de profundis* perspective, in the queer reality of queer depression. In this peculiar space, one is silent and does not *make* sense, being "absent from other people's meaning" (Kristeva 4). It is only possible to describe one's depression when the depression is already gone, since "in this beginning of otherness. . . lacking the filter of language, [one] cannot inscribe [one's] violence in 'no,' nor any other sign. [One] can expel it only by means of gestures, spasms or shouts" (Kristeva 15). In depression, one is always beyond comprehension.

The crisis house: A Remedy?

> The first time was because of my tongue, the way it settled in my
> mouth like a slug, silent and glistening. The sun shone in squares
> through the dirty window and I sat in stasis on the green couch for
> hours, forfeit to gravity, all my molecules engorged and motionless.
>
> The second time was because we'd fought about something that I forget
> and I cried and cried and I couldn't stop crying even in my psychia-
> trist's office I cried and couldn't speak and he told me that if I didn't
> speak he'd have to put me in the hospital and I didn't want to go there
> so I said No and he called the crisis house. . .
> . . . I wailed like a child and I cried and I
> cried and I cried
> as generous and impersonal as rain (Mayor, "Crisis House" 27)

The "Crisis House" is where the depressive muteness and the depressive spasm compete for hegemony. Therefore, in depression one does not do things oneself: one is being worried about, one is being taken care of, and one is being treated. Depression is "irreversible on its own" (Kristeva 10). A crisis house is where one is taken when one is not depressive enough to be hospitalized. A crisis house provides one with peace and pills. Contrary to the description of the "house in crisis" in "Continue," the crisis house—this intermediary place between "normality" and "abnormality"—is orderly and logical:

> This is an ordinary house, plastered
> with a calm mask of white stucco.
> This house is flanked with other white
> houses trimmed in blue, green, or red.
> . . . This is a mundane house with a large
> bay window clouded with curtains like
> cataracts. . . .
>
> This is a tidy house with a prim green
> lawn, eschewing window boxes,
> unadorned. This is a house you drive
> past every day and do not see.
> This is a house where you are incapable
> of looking up.
>
> This is a house that squats stupidly and says
> nothing. This is a house with eavestroughs
> full of spiders. This is a house that models
> banality and flaunts its ordered shingles
> to the neighbours. ("Crisis House" 29-30)

The crisis house resembles other houses; at first sight, it is by no means unique. Still, it is a house that is invisibly contaminated; it secretly hosts spiders and cataracts. It is not inherently peaceful, but temporarily pacified. Even though the crisis house allows depression, or, rather, depression is prerequisite for one to become its inhabitant (owing to which trait the house—seemingly—is capable of providing the soothing sense that the anxiety of fitting nowhere is groundless), the woman "contained" in it is still driven towards fragmentation and disintegration. In depression, one is always ready for "a plunge into death"; the poetic reverie of the "house in crisis" is the festival of death drive. The homoerotic, Canadian, female speaking I, is already triply absent; the very fact that she *does* exist is queer—and, in the context of the inspection carried out—doubly *queer*.

Rebuilding the House: Convalescence

When left alone, the queer speaking I in Mayor's poem smothers the light-bulb in her blanket:

> . . . I unbundle
> the blanket and the shattered glass rasps against itself
> in a small opaque mosaic. There's a picture, there's a message,
> there's a narrative that emerges from this fragmentation and it
> whispers *touch me touch me touch me* and trembling
> I answer *yes*. My arms are so cooperative, the veins throwing
> themselves against the skin, urging liberation, urging passion,
> the long sharp pain, hair line thin, the indrawn breadth. ("Crisis House" 33)

In this orderly, mute interior, what the woman reads, comprehends and lives, are fragmentation and disorder, by means of which she "[pieces herself] together inside out" (Mayor 33). The opening in her skin is her re-entry to the wilderness: "This is what it's like inside a waterfall, the torrent in your ears,/the rolling of your body over rocks and rapids" (Mayor 33). The heroine of the reverie desires death, but the suicidal act is—in fact—a non-act: "it is only what I wish I'd done, my secret,/sweet and warm, my scarred and veteran fictions" (Mayor 34). A self in crisis is "*as if* dead, [can only be] *playing* dead [reenacting some individual] "poetics of survival," an inverted life, coiled around imaginary and real disintegration to the extent of embodying death *as if* it were real" (Kristeva 73). Mayor's *queer* self in crisis is a *living* corpse that emerges, thanks to the anguish, "out of nothingness" (Kristeva 73), and into a reality beyond *true* meaning and *true* feeling, into an imperfect, but *definable*, and thus inhabitable space.

Therefore, even though the crisis house is "ordinary," "mundane," and "stupid," it is simultaneously "a blessing, benediction." Powerfully *there,* it "welcomes you like a mouth/and caresses you like swallowing" (35). The walls of the crisis house are "a blanket to cover yourself" (35). This is the place one returns to, a place that returns one to the *texted* world: in depression one is meaningless to the world, and at the same time, the world is meaningless to one. In queer, Canadian, feminine depression—the meaninglessness is triple. As remedy, the crisis house provides an "identification [which] insures the subject's entrance into the universe of signs and creation" (Kristeva 23): it *is* there, it does not *become.*

Case Closed?

O'Grady, writing about the queer African femininity, whose motto provides a maverick keynote to my musings on the queer selves of Chandra Mayor's characters, agrees with Germaine Warkentin, who, pondering upon Canadianness, writes that for the sake of self definition "we need, if nothing else, an image in a mirror." Invisibility might give one a "special angle of vision," an "outside-within stance," which, nevertheless, transforms one into nothing but an unusual observer. One's unusual observations can be acknowledged only when they are spoken out, or written down. The crisis house, the queer space, the intermediary between the definitions, offering its patient a substitute I, makes it possible for one who lacks a homogenous identity, to return to the meaningful reality.

Notes

1. "Gale, hurricanes, and downpours haunt the *Poetics of Space*, all vicissitudes that make the simplest of simple huts shine in strength of sheltering. Storm makes sense of shelter, and if the shelter is sound, the shelter makes the surrounding storm good, enjoyable, re-creational, something that Bachelard uses to open his understanding of house and universe, of intimacy and immensity. Always container, sometimes contained, the house serves Bachelard as the portal to metaphors of imagination" (Stilgoe viii).

Works Cited

Atwood, Margaret. "Through the One-Way Mirror." *Images. Canada Through Literature*. Ed. John Borovilos. Scaroborough, Ontario: Prentice Hall Ginn Canada, 1996.
Bachelard, Gaston. *The Poetics of Reverie*. Boston: Beacon Press, 1971.
———. *The Poetics of Space*. Boston: Beacon Press, 1994.

Felman, Shoshana. "Women and Madness: the Critical Phallacy." *The Feminist Reader*. Ed. Catherine Belsey and Jane Moore. London: Macmillam Press, 1997.

Hammonds, Evelynn. "Black (W)holes and the Geometry of Black Female Sexuality." *Feminism and 'Race.'* Ed. Kum-Kum Bhavani. Oxford: Oxford University Press, 2000.

Kristeva, Julia. *Black Sun: Depression and Melancholia*. New York: Columbia University Press, 1989.

Mayor, Chandra. "The Crisis House." *August Witch*. Winnipeg: Cyclops Press, 2002.

Monk, Katherine. Weird Sex & Snowshoes and Other Canadian Film Phenomena. Vancouver: Raincoast Books, 2001.

Pouchard, Line. "Queer Desire in The Well of Loneliness." *The Feminist Reader*. Ed. Catherine Belsey and Jane Moore. London: Macmillam Press Ltd., 1997.

Stilgoe John R. Foreword. *The Poetics of Space*. By Gaston Bachelard. Boston: Beacon Press, 1994.

JUST A STAGE? BIPHOBIA IN THEORY AND PRACTICE

ANNA BORGOS

> Have you heard about the idea that a female and a male self can be found in everyone? Thus, it may sound logical that we are looking for two people at once. Our female self is looking for the male one, and vice versa. Perhaps bisexuality can be better understood this way.
>
> I think when you fall in love, then it's the other's being, mind, feelings, taste, humor that you love, and this has nothing to do with sex. Of course the body is also important, but since I'm not left cold by either the female nor the male body, I think it's all the same whether whom I love is a boy or a girl. And then it's her/him who is there, and I don't need anyone else for sex.
>
> (Extracts from an internet forum, "What's the matter with bis?")

This paper tries to explore some possible roots and potential consequences of the phenomenon of biphobia, connecting the theoretical outlines with some experiences I've got in the Hungarian LGBT "community."

The above quotations indicate that the rhetoric on bisexuality is closely intertwined with the different arguments on the concept of identity in general. Conscious or subconscious standpoints about gender identities have their implications regarding the status of and the attitudes towards bisexuality, too. In one major system of ideas, bisexuality is approached in a framework where sexes, gender identities and sexual orientations are considered clearcut and stable categories. In this framework, bisexuality may represent a disturbing phenomenon, but also another group that needs to be represented and included in sexual minorities. From a different point of view, however, it can be approached outside of this structure, used for subverting the system of sex- (gender-) based identities. The first group of opinions seems typical for a (semi-) politicized LBGTcommunity, while the second viewpoint is based more on post-structuralist theoretical grounds. I attempt to explore these major discourses that determine the sub-discourses on bisexuality and to raise the question whether there are potential passages between them.

* * *

How can bisexuality be placed in the framework of the political movements of sexual minorities? These movements are built on a need of acknowledgment and representation, in a situation of invisibility and prohibition. The "ethnic model" of identity politics—either in a liberal, equality-centered or a radical, difference-centered way—expresses a psychological need for being reinforced, with reference to or in opposition with an oppressing majority, creating its own institutions, forums, events, etc. While it might result in an isolated, "underground" being, it provides a safe space; separation indicates a need and a constraint at the same time. This bond strongly exists, since prohibiting and tabooing are strongly existing too. It is basically prohibition and discrimination that produces and stabilizes identities (Foucault), which are supposed to provide a reassuring force. From a "primary," psychological aspect, these spaces and ways of representation seem to be essential.

As for the situation of gays and lesbians in Hungary, they are generally in a "pre-identical," partly in an identity-vindicating state. What most LGBT-identified people have to face, is the difficulty or impossibility of coming-out. This results either in a closeted being, or an occasional immersing in a hidden and separated "gay world." Organizing gay and lesbian communities, festivals, associations (without even including "bisexual and transgender" in their names) reinforces the sense of difference along the line of sexuality, while it helps to break out of the closet.

Since it is the (op)position that creates a community which is otherwise not homogenous at all, the different sub-identities which stand outside the most direct interests—among them bisexuality—are often put aside. These omitted groups then create their own identity politics that claims to represent sub-identities with their special interests. This is beginning to happen in Hungary too, mostly on the level of naming groups, festivals or publications, and usually in terms of including the term "lesbian." The representation of bisexuality is rarely an issue. The gay magazine calls itself the only gay magazine in Hungary (while stressing that it is open for lesbians too; bisexuality is basically not thematized). After ten years, "Gay and Lesbian Film and Cultural Festival" included in its name "Bisexual." The biggest LGBT organization is called Háttér Society for LGBT People in English, but its Hungarian name is Háttér Society for Gays – although its subtitle contains that it works for the equality of LGBT minorities protecting human rights and providing human services.

Bisexuality is frequently considered a "pre-identity" state, merely a sexual practice without any other personal or political commitment. This approach to bisexuality is probably the major root for biphobia both among gays and straights. The stereotypes around them indicate a strong defense of the boundaries of identities and sexual orientations. The dichotomized sexuality assumes everyone straight in a straight world, and everyone gay in a gay community, which maintains the almost total invisibility of bisexuals. Within this straight/gay dichotomization it seems much more difficult to come out as bisexual, especially to reclaim a bisexual identity or history (Garber). Often bisexuals themselves don't consider their bisexuality more than a sexual habit. But for many of them, facing the social expectations (in many ways different among straights and gays), the internalized fears, may cause a similar identity crisis to what gays and lesbians often go through. It is not just the sexes, between which the shift takes places, but also between levels of acceptability and visibility.

I've done a "micro-study," on the basis of two Hungarian internet forums discussing bisexuality. It is remarkable that the discussion basically consists of arguments "pro" or "contra" bisexuality. The opinions are diverse, with some recurrent motifs either from the "defending" or the "opposing" side. One major group of opinions associates bisexuality with sex-centrism, polygamy or promiscuity, emotional and sexual infidelity and irresponsibility. They take it for granted that bisexuality means parallel relationships with men and women.

> ("Lesbian space") I have a bad opinion about bis perhaps because I've had very negative experiences with them so far. Their sense of morality, in general is under the ass of the frog. The other thing is that bis are usually not reliable, they are much looser in sex too.

> ("What's the matter with bis?") Bisexuality excludes fidelity from the beginning. If you have a woman, sooner or later some guy also appears in the picture, if you have a husband, male friend, lover, etc, then you need a woman on the side. . .

Another, very typical train of thought, often within the same contributions, goes on by declaring that bisexuality does not exist at all. According to these views, this is just a transitional stage, an incapacity for making up one's mind on one side or the other. A temporary excuse, a "developing step" for compromisers or beginners, or a trendy excursion for straights, who may return to the shelter and social privileges of the straight world at any time. These speakers seem to know what bisexuals "really" are—either this or that, either straights or "stone-fags." There are two options altogether, and one has to decide between them; there is a wall that one cannot just walk through in either direction. These remarks indicate a kind of "internalized heterophobia" or an idea of "compulsory homosexuality" that sees any connection with the opposite sex as non-sense:

> Another thing is that I don't believe in bisexuality from the beginning. Bis think that they are bis since they have orgasm with women and pricks too, while it doesn't mean anything. And I can't imagine to be in love with a woman and a man at once. It's rather some transitional stage.
>
> According to my observations, when someone goes out with a boy and a girl, there is always some trick. Most of my bi acquaintances turned to be "stone-fag" or they just tried the same-sex in the name of some sexual libertinism.
>
> By the way, in my modest opinion and (not few) experiences bisexuality doesn't exist. I would rather call it a middle stage in a developmental process that leads to homosexuality. When you can't tell, explain, admit either to yourself or to others what the hell you want.

Other remarks suggest that it is a more complex, emotionally saturated state that is, however, more difficult to grasp or represent than either straight or gay identity—which bisexuals themselves suffer from:

> I think that you have the same problem with everything that is not concrete. I mean if you don't belong to either group, at least you are unable to classify yourself somewhere, then the community will not accept you either.
>
> So do I have to pursue a decision? Certainty? Declaration?—so that I can belong to a real group at last, and be reconciled?

Over the pro and con arguments, some talkers try to get closer to the phenomenon, which soon raises questions and uncertainties about defining what bisexuality is, where it "begins," whether it has grades, whether it is a sexual practice or a lifestyle. The incapacity and the constraint of categorizing themselves along the lines of sexual orientation bring about great discomfort.

> I try to find out from what point we can speak about bisexuality. Am I bisexual if I'm concerned about sex with a same-sex person? Or only in case of the acceptance of a same-sex partnership in everyday life (this I'm not thinking about at all, in fact I find the idea repulsive).

One of the participants does not rise to the defence of bisexuality, but thinks the institution of monogamy itself is precarious. S/he sees the main root of biphobia in the compulsory need to possess and at the same time classify others.

> I think when people rail against bisexuality, they insist on thinking about a partnership in the framework of property relations. Bisexuality, in their view, can't be put in this framework. And for non-bisexuals you can figure out simplifying definitions, while for bisexes it's hard to find one attribute that would cover them properly. This is why it's not possible to talk about bisexual rights, while in the case of gay rights it seems possible.

I also made a quick and non-representative survey among the members of Háttér Society for Gays and Lesbians. This included questions regarding the stability, exactness and relevance of the subjects' sexual orientation, their personal attitudes to bisexuals, and their perception of the attitudes of others. The answers reflect upon the stereotypes rather than display them. People perceive the difficult status, the stereotypical refusal or invisibility of bisexuality within the gay community. They acknowledge that it is not an issue within the organization either, while it has several bisexual members. I will return to some of these opinions later.

* * *

The above processes and ideas can be seen in a different light from the ground of (de)construtivist theories. This theoretical standpoint—with potential consequences for the possible political actions, too—taking its roots primarily from Judith Butler's works suggests that identity-based politics, instead of superseeding marginalization, actually works to reinforce it. Postulating a repressed and homogenized identity that should be discovered, acknowledged and represented, may resolve some obvious inequities, but while doing that, conceals other fundamental questions. By claiming an independent identity, we can reverse or struggle with an oppressive gaze, but we cannot back out of it and replace our muted or distorted identities with a real and authentic one. Fixing an autonomous identity always presumes a fixation of the "interpellating Other" (Althusser), a "respon[se] to a request" (Butler, "Imitation" 13). Paradoxically: the moment of subjection necessarily implies oppression.

A typical symptom of a two-folded discourse that reduces and at the same time reinforces the marginal status of sexual minorities is the popular habit of asking "experts" about the issue of "homosexuality." A well-known psychologist in Hungary has recently been asked about the possible effects of the education program of Labrisz Association. ("What is the standpoint of science in connection with [homosexuality and education]?") The expert commented on the program in a basically supportive and liberal way; his rhetoric, however, is deeply typical of the relation to sexual "otherness." Quoting him: "Informing the youth about sexuality [sic], including the knowledge on homosexuality, is very important. . . . Homosexuality is an attribute we are born with, and in no way can it be changed during the lifecourse. So there is no danger of the mis-education of children in this field" ("'Ma már" ["Today we think. . . "] 10). All this suggests that "homosexuality" (the medical term is not an accident either), as an inborn thing, can be defined and described in opposition to the norm. There is no danger; the condition is not infectious; homosexuals will remain a minority forever. There is something that is "responsible" for this alteration, this is why they are different from "us," obviously including me, the expert. But what about heterosexuality, who explores the genes or social effects causing straightness? Not to speak about bisexuality and other "deformed" sexualities. For the expert's opinion also suggests a polarization of the world for straights and gays; but it is the straights who make the division putting gays into a controllable category of "minority."

On the other hand, while (or since) identity is produced from difference, it also carries multiple differences in itself. Differences and contradictions are emerging not just between identities, but also *within* them (Fuss). Since the *relation* between the self and the prevailing "Other" is multiple, identity cannot be grasped and fixed either, it slips out of our hands. When we try to make it fixed and unified, we ignore a couple of further differences. Not because individual experiences are so diverse and so individual, but rather because the self-other relation, the constructedness is so multiple. It is the politics of this constructedness that is really interesting—the process, in which representation and identity mutually and continuously reflect and produce each other.

Gender identities and sexual orientations represent a field where this contingency and constructedness are very easy to ignore. Naturalizing mechanisms that strive to essentialize the role of sexes or erotic attractions, and to make them coinciding elements, work strongly from all sides. This approach does not reckon with the complex ways of sexual bondings that cannot be expressed in the prevailing categories. "There are no direct expressive or causal lines between sex, gender, gender presentation, sexual practice, fantasy and sexuality" (Butler, "Imitation" 25). This makes categorization impossible and unnecessary, based on the assumption that the different subject positions should not be multiplied, but need to be destroyed or subverted. Instead of a "strategic essentialism," we should choose a strategic provisionality. This does not necessarily lead to the depolitization of LGBT efforts, but rather points out that an identity-based politics could (should?) be followed by a politics of identity-disruption. To consciously show the constructedness and (compulsory) performativity might be a starting point for an opposing strategy. As Jane Gallop puts it: "Identity must be continually assumed and immediately called into question" (Gallop xii). Or quoting a similar remark from Elaine Marks: "There must be a sense of identity, even though it would be fictitious" (Marks 110). Referring to Butler's vocabulary, gender is a performance, an imitation which has no original version. Butler makes it graspable with an Aretha Franklin song, saying: "You make me feel like a natural woman. . . " She is captivated by the idea that this "you" has endless possible versions: "What if she were singing it to a drag queen, whose performance somehow confirmed her own?" (Butler, "Imitation" 27-28).

If identity itself is not identical and stable, but a contingent, unclear and temporary field, then instead of being a firm base, it might become a destabilizing force. After a certain point difficulties may emerge in deciding on what basis, in the name of whom and for whom we want to speak. This argument frequently comes up in implicit or explicit ways within the "community" when organizing a social event, editing a book or staging a public demonstration.

The complicated issue of representation has recently been raised in Hungary in connection with a commercial TV program. In one of the two newly aired reality shows, a gay man and a lesbian woman were selected, and then voted into the show by the audience. The characters receive mixed reactions from part of the viewers and the media. But there are big debates also within the gay community, basically on the question whether these people should represent "us," whether they are the right ones and this is the "proper" form of representation. Some state that this kind of mission cannot be expected from them, while others say that they are doing it anyway, whether it is their intention or not, at least in the eyes of the millions who watch them. Apart from the inevitably biased media selection procedure of choosing characters who strongly reflect the general stereotypes, it is equally problematic to decide from the "inside," who can represent "us" and how to show what we are really like. It is probably only a diversity of representations that could equilibrate the biases or constraints.

To narrow the question to bisexuality: aversions in this context are not directed to bisexuality or bisexual people, but the identity-based and identity-creating politics itself. From this point of view, the contingency and precarious status of bisexuality is not a limitation, but a potential not to consider it an identity that needs to be recognized, a phenomenon that may help to challenge the very dichotomies of sexual orientations and the prominent role of sexes in erotic attraction (Esterberg; Jagose). *The "mission" therefore is not to justify that bisexuality is more than just a stage, but to show that identity in general is "just a stage," in every sense.*

For some people, calling themselves bisexual is more a political statement than a sexual practice (as for others, or on other occasions naming themselves gay or lesbian might have the same effect), through which they can designate the potentiality and contingency of sexual orientations and practices themselves. This is close to a kind of "post-identical," queer state that imagines sexuality in much more complex ways, along much more diverse axes than sex or sexual orientation. This is a less typical attitude among LGBT people in Hungary, whether politically active or not. Among the members of Háttér, there were only two people (two women) who represented an attitude of this kind. One of them—answering the question "To what extent do you feel the category of your sexual orientation to be a stable, exact and relevant one?" wrote the following:

> I don't think that identity necessarily reflects sexual practice. I can imagine being attracted to a man, but for this I won't define myself as bi- or heterosexual.

This answer suggests that sexual orientation might have parts that overlook the sex of the actual partner. Another answer to the same question specifies some cases when the person consciously chooses the category she identifies with. It seems to be at least as much a political gesture as a personal one:

> I'm a lesbian, but at some moments, when I'm pissed off by biphobia, I call myself bisexual. I'm not attracted to men though, and usually it's easier to essentialize. It's not very subtle, as in many ways I don't have much in common with a couple of lesbians. But for the outside world this is a relevant category. There are moments when you cannot specify too much—e.g. speaking with a homophobic creature or a rushing politician.

Her answer to another question, regarding the definition of bisexuality, reflects upon the potential and vague character of it:

> Bisexuality may refer to someone who can feel attracted to any gender. But it's difficult to define, as there may be people like that, who still don't call themselves bisexual. There is a kind of future-potential in it, I feel. That is, I think someone bisexual if s/he says that s/he can be attracted to any gender at present, or thinks it possible in the future.

Some years ago, several people in Hungary founded the "Group of Genderless People" (NINCS). Its ideology basically coincides with a radical Butlerian standpoint, denying biological states as the bases of gender roles.

Here are some excerpts from the NINCS "Reader":

> It is a mistake to think that one is attracted to some (of the) sexes. There are a lot of attributes of the other among which anatomic sex is only one. When we are in love, we are usually not tied to the genitals of the other, but to the whole person. Therefore it is a false idea to consider someone hetero/homo/bi/a/poli/etc.-sexual. The term "sexual orientation" is compelled into/impressed on? our mind in order to fix, observe, manipulate and exploit our personality. . .
>
> The real challenge for "normality," that is heterosexual dictatorship, is so-called bisexuality. There is a great helplessness regarding its status on the part of those affected, "normal people" and "homosexuals" too. Who is the bisexual? A "normal person" who is winding down a bit and wants to have fun? Or a gay person who partly submits to the norms?
>
> It would be best if gays did not practice their sexuality as gays. If we had no word for that, if it was not an issue at all. Gay liberation is harmful in this sense, as it reinforces this self-consciousness. It is not the gays who need to be liberated, because then they will always remain the group that can be oppressed in different ways. (Juhász)

Gay discourse, according to the NINCS activists, reinforces the scale between two extremes, homo- and heterosexuality. It does not assume that people may interpret their sexuality *regardless* of the sex of their partner. They see as a success that we can choose between homo-, hetero- and bisexuality, but insist that choosing is obligatory. They give a lucid example of an alternative choice:

> Say someone is attracted to fat people. S/he is looking for her pregnant mother in every partner, together with the power and safety that the mother used to provide. Therefore s/he falls in love and has sex with fat men, because their social roles and appearance represent the attributes s/he is looking for. One day s/he meets a lesbian woman who is strong, protective—and fat. Falls in love with her. Can we say that this person is either hetero- or homosexual? Does the term "bisexual" tell us anything significant about his/her sexuality? (Kuszing, "Buzológia")

The group does not exist anymore, and although it made an impact in certain circles, it did not really influence "mainstream" activism. It did not have a real scope of social or political activities, and the queer conception swallowed the marginalized sexual identities that still needed to be represented and acknowledged. Since then, another association, Habeas Corpus Workteam has been established by more or less the same people. HCW, taking into account the prevailing gender system, is doing serious and widespread work for discriminated LGBT-s, as well as abused women and children.

Finally, I would like to quote from one of the leaflets of NINCS—a construction that by repeating and exaggerating the most typical stereotypes, shows the absurdity of the "how one became . . . sexual" type of questions. The text, entitled "John Smith: A Bisexual" (Kuszing, "Kovács János"), is a fictive autobiography, an identity-fiction that exposes the fictitious nature of identity through a parodically compiled narrative built around the protagonist's sexual behaviour:

> I was born in 10 May 1973. My mother loved me very much, she always warned me against dangerous things, wouldn't let me climb a tree, and told me not to play soccer, because it is rude, and this is why I became a bisexual. I say I'm bisexual because I don't dare to admit that I'm actually homosexual. For there are no bisexuals, I think; people are attracted either to men or women. . .

The inconsistent and controversial mixture of arguments are going on the same way, providing a tool for rewriting and revealing the arbitrary rhetoric on the process of gender identification.

The two planes—to put it simply: identity politics and the politics of identity subversion—may have meeting points. Identity politics is probably "just a stage," too, and probably an inevitable one. The struggle for the liberation of identities might be followed by a struggle for the liberation *from* identities. If discrimination is not a problem any more, then the need for a declared identity and a safe sub-culture will also be less urgent. This does not necessarily involve a total assimilation and depolitization; to reflect upon the consequences that identity itself is a stage, would perhaps make possible a more mature identity politics, which takes into account the needs and necessities as well as the casual and constructed "nature" of identities.

Works Cited

Althusser, Louis. *Essays on Ideology*. London: Verso, 1984.
Butler, Judith. Bodies That Matter: On the Discursive Limits of "Sex." New York: Routledge, 1993.
———. Gender Trouble: Feminism and the Subversion of Identity. New York: Routledge, 1990.
———. "Imitation and Gender Insubordination." *Inside/Out. Lesbian Theories, Gay Theories*. Ed. Diana Fuss. New York: Routledge, 1991.
Esterberg, Kristin G. Lesbian and Bisexual Identities. Constructing Communities, Constructing Selves. Philadelphia: Temple UP, 1997.
Foucault, Michel. *A szexualitás története*. Budapest: Atlantisz, 1998.
Fuss, Diana. Essentially Speaking. Feminism, Nature and Difference. New York: Routledge, 1989.
Gallop, Jane. The Daughter's Seduction. Feminism and Psychoanalysis. Ithaca: Cornell UP, 1982.
Garber, Marjorie. Vice Versa. Bisexuality and the Eroticism of Everyday Life. London: Penguin Books, 1997.

Jagose, Annamarie. *Queer Theory. An Introduction.* New York: New York UP, 1996.
Juhász, Géza. A Reader of NINCS. Manuscript, 1996.
Kuszing, Gábor. "Buzológia, avagy a tökfejű tehén esete." [Fagology, or the Case of the Blockhead Cow.] Manuscript, 1997.
―――. "Kovács János biszexuális." [John Smith: A Bisexual.] Manuscript, 1998.
"Lesbian space" internet forum <www.pride.hu>.
"Ma már másképp gondolkozunk." Beszélgetés Ranschburg Jenővel ["Today We Think Differently." An Interview with Jenő Ranschburg]. *Köznevelés* 28 (2002).
Marks, Elaine. "Feminism's Wake." *Boundary 2* 12.2 (1984): 99-110.
"What's the matter with bis?" internet forum <www.pride.hu>.

THE CITADEL PARK. A SPECIFIC NODE IN A NETWORK FOR (QUEER) DESIRE

ELS DE VOS

Introduction

Parks have a gendered connotation which is constructed by the reciprocal relations between the space and the use of the space. This paper focuses on the Citadel Park in Ghent, Belgium, known as a favourite meeting place for male homo- and bisexuals, who have very specific ways of using, discovering and experiencing the hilly park. By doing library research complemented by two months of empirical observations and interviews with park visitors during the summer of 2002, I identified several spatial patterns based on the manner in which people use and experience the park. The division of the park into two levels, a lower and an upper level, is for example particularly significant, because, given the more outspoken appropriation of the upper level by homosexuals, tells something about the reason why he is visiting the park. Also the distance which the park visitor has to travel from home, can tell something about the way the visitor deals with the significance of public and private space. This paper is interested in the interplay between the physical morphology and history of the park and the significance and the usage by different park visitors, especially gay men. It wants to contribute to the understanding of how public space mediates between men with a queer desire and straight visitors. At the end I give some suggestions about the recommended development for the park.

Romantic park or a dangerous jungle?

With its 2500 acres, the Citadel Park is the biggest urban park of Ghent. However, 700 acres are occupied by buildings (Deherdt, Deseyn and Van Den Hole 59). This green "island" is located in the south of Ghent near the motorway. The park is cut off from the surrounding residential neighbourhoods by busy roads. The mainly English landscape style of the park and the amalgam of monuments and elements (caves, pergolas, music kiosk, rose-gardens, cascades, etc.) are intended to seduce the "romantic visitor." There are also some elements of a French landscape style: a few gardens with a strict rectilinear geometry and carefully monitored hierarchy, and an axis through the park. From the hilltop the visitor can see the entire park. Many people enjoy the beautiful environment "I prefer this park for its 'closed' skyline. By that I mean that you see green everywhere, and not immediately the surrounding cars and buildings," comments one female visitor. The hills, colossal buildings with blind spots, obscure caves and tortuous paths give the park, experienced from the "ground level," a labyrinth-like character.

A military history

The park is named after the former Citadel that was built in 1823 on one of the highest points of the city. That strategic fortification served a site for masculine activity: handling war, defending the city and accommodating soldiers. Remnants, such as remainders of casemates and bunkers, still testify to that military past. Fifty years after the building of the Citadel, the exterior parts of the fortification were demolished and replaced by a park "à l'Anglaise." About 1877, several rock gardens and formations were laid out. The biggest rock/cave is called the "Swiss valley." Later, there came a music kiosk, a Museum of the Fine Arts, and a playground for children. Ponds, surrounded by a "promenade" in a hilly landscape give it a romantic atmosphere. In preparation for the world exhibition of 1913 the Floraliën Hal was built and the rose-gardens were planted. In the "hot greenhouse" an aerodrome was installed in 1920. The rough landscape evolved into a park with a great diversity of flowers. Besides the layout of rock gardens and flowerbeds, the paths were broadened to accommodate the tastes and wishes of the increasing crowd. Paul Bergmans, Jacques de Lalaing and Louis Minard are some of the artists from the Victorian Age who lent their names to the lanes and paths in the park. Female names are absent. Most of the statues honour men: Edmond van Beveren, Emile Claus, Oswald de Kerchove or king Boudewijn; or symbolise the masculine: the "Big Lion," the "Fighting tigers," etc. The design of the park also carries masculine connotations. This is to be expected, considering the fact that the park was built in a society where men were the most important actors. For the centenary of 1930 the park was renovated a second time. In 1940 the "Conch," an open air theatre, was built and in 1963 the so called "Garden of Ghent" had to give way to a new hall. The International Congress Centrum (ICC) came in 1975. About 1900 the park was said to be frequented by a mixed public, as the several shelters for walkers indicate. Also during the world exhibition and centenary the park was visited by a diverse public. The demission of the park-keeper in 1960 has turned this evolution, according to a neighbouring senior (Libert 1999). From then on the park attracted other subgroups, like homosexuals. The masculine connotations returned in a transformed way.

Mixed use?

Seeing the fact that the park is situated on the route from the station to the city centre, it is crossed by passengers, men or women, on foot or bike. Actually, all kinds of people visit the park: seniors, parents with their children, youth, people doing sports and museum visitors. Some walk their dogs; others take a walk, feed the ducks or just look for some company on one of the benches. Young women on their own are quite exceptional; men on their own are common. The Citadel Park is also a meeting place for homosexual and bisexual men. The distinction between the two is not always very clear, as the literature indicates (Sioen, 21, Van Gemert 171). One gay visitor I spoke to, report it like this: "Your belief in relations, marriage, monogamy and the hetero/homo division is totally broken down. If you walk in the park and a bit later in the city, then you see the so called 'gays' with their girlfriend or wife walking hand in hand in the shopping street." There are also those who are still "closeted." Some gay men meet each other here with anonymous sexual contact in mind. That then happens in rooms or in the bushes of the park. Along one street surrounding the park, also some boys prostitutes are working. What makes this park so attractive for gay men? Does their presence change the public character of the park? Is their a privacy gradient in the park?

Node in a network of spaces with a homosexual preference

The Citadel Park is part of the network of meeting places based on a queer desire.[1] Not only parks, but also specific cinemas, discotheques, hotels, restaurants and parking places along motorways are well known among gays from the oral tradition, Internet, and guides. The network around Brussels includes, for example, the Central station, Park du Bruxelles and the Park du Cinquantenaire (Sioen 21). "The Citadel Park is quoted high in the International Gay Magazine. You can notice this every night. They come from far for a friend. You can tell from the licence plates," says a neighbor. The international character must be contextualised, as the following witness indicates: "I mostly walk, because I live nearby [at one and a half kilometres]. Many people come by car. That is the fastest way when they come from Flanders. I think that many people park their car in the area and then come on foot for the sake of discretion. Not many people come by bike. Some are just cycling through, the "I want to, but I'm afraid-types." The cars come from Bruges, Courtrai and Ostend. There are many people from West-Flanders, Antwerp and Brussels have their own scene! Sint-Niklaas and Aalst are on the edge. Many just come for a visit after work, after having drunk something with friends. Few just come for the sole purpose of visiting the park!" The attainability of the park by car and the parking space around and in the park is an important factor for the success of the park among gays. "The car, as both an instrument and a location, a lonely bubble and a protected shelter, a physical implement and a moving vision, a mass-produced object and a personal space, might be the ultimate icon of cruising" (Aaron 148).

The boy prostitutes work along the cycling paths at the Leopold-I lane. "That is very normal," indicates a visitor. "They are easily seen from the street. There is a wide footpath, a strip of grass, a cycling path and from there on there is a hill. The whole is well lit. And in front of that there are parking places. It's a perfect place to pick up people or to disappear into the bushes on the hill." At the ends of the road drivers can use the roundabouts to easily access the street again. The lane is also the quietest surrounding street, so gays feel comfortable there.

The act of looking

Although the homosexual community has built up a series of "facilities," until recently they have been ignored by the urban sociology and urban planning (Duyves 74). Their presence, though it undeniably marks the city, is yet almost unnoticeable and seems physically absent. Lesbians are still less visible. They have, unlike gays, no custom of visiting squares or woods. "Sexually, these sites are not interesting to them, but the main reason is the different attitude of women. They are much more focussed on the relational than on the sexual aspect," according to a lesbian participant in a youth queer association in Ghent. Only some insider-bars and posters of lesbian organisations give away their presence. The "invisibility" of queers can undoubtedly be explained by the oppression in the past and the taboo that was imposed on them. Considering the fact that homosexuality wasn't accepted in the past,[2] homosexuals needed to develop a series of tactics to meet companions without being noticed by the police (Chauncey and Miller 223-277).

Cruising is an insider's term among gays. Queer men walk trough the park in order to seduce somebody. By walking very slowly and carefully looking around them, they scan the environment in order to find potential candidates. The act of looking is crucial. By looking at someone a bit longer than is usual, cruisers show their preference. The following quote explains this very well: "If someone looks at you with a lingering look, and looks away, and then looks at you again. If you looked at a straight man he wouldn't stare back, he'd look immediately away" (Chauncey and Miller 239).

Women in the park are totally ignored by gays, as if they were "non people."[3] This is the cruisers' way to show respect for women, as if they want to say "we don't want to bother you." Because they are for the rest attentively peering, this attitude evokes discomfort in many women. They do not feel safe under those "staring eyes," even if the gazes are not aimed at them. It may be that the discomfort originates with women being used to being looked at. In many "straight" men, however, the "seducing gaze" evokes an even greater uneasiness. They feel like "prey," caught by the voluptuousness of the man-gaze. This situation can best be compared to the voyeuristic gaze that women often face (Hirsch, *Tel-Aviv* 66). Gay men "took full advantage of the cultural injunction against men looking at other men in the same sexually assertive way they gazed at women; a 'normal' man almost automatically averted his eyes if they happened to lock with those of a stranger" (Chauncey and Miller 239). Why does the park allow so easily such a way of looking? Where exactly in the park cruising takes place?

The cruising-circuit

Although the use of space based on homosexual preference actually takes place in the whole park, nevertheless there are certain rules, as indicated by one man I interviewed. "There are some circuits. One passes by the little pool. There are different interesting elements: there are some benches where something can happen. There is also the cave with the cascade. That's a very good place, and you are very well hidden. The top of that cave is also a very good place. There is a little bench and you are protected by the rock behind you. You are sitting high up and can see whoever is coming. Another circuit goes up the 'ills.' A little path takes you up, and then you arrive between all those little bushes. It's very dark there at night, so that's an ideal place to make things happen. You can see shadows there. But those shadows do things. That circuit goes around the theatre up to the top of the 'Swiss valley.' Also there anything can happen."

He continues: "Also on the summit of the other smaller cave—or no, it's more like an arch—something can be seen. There you can follow between the bushes a little path that goes up. It doesn't go further as far as I know. In any case I don't go further. Well, there are gay men walking everywhere, but as far as I know, things only happen in this part of the park. That makes sense, because it's the part that is best hidden between the bushes." The interesting points are strategic places. They make it possible for men to have a good view. At the same time other people can't see them very well. Geographically it is remarkable that hetero-couples stay downstairs, whereas "gentlemen's love" is only taking place in the hills, according to an interviewee. Of course the division isn't so clear. But we can say that the place is more indicative than the activity. The division of the hilly park into two levels, a lower level and an upper level, is particularly significant. Given the more direct appropriation of the upper level by homosexuals, the "upper level" of the park can be considered as a level for gay activities.

The path parallel to the Théodore Canneelpath is the "main cruising street." It is secluded with bushes on either, which produces a tunnel-like effect that framed the exchanged glimpses. Walking down that path, one passes flirting men. The difference between this scene and a scene of heterosexual prostitution is that those men choose to cruise and to be cruised. This way they are "clients" and "merchandise" at the same time. They investigate and allow themselves to be investigated. This duality generates a tangible tension. The bushes increase the tension because they can hide people. "There is something strange about the park. You want to meet people there and at the same time you don't want to meet people there. Or no, it's more like this: you want to see people, but they mustn't see you," comments a regularly cruising man.

The night as ultimate wrap or metaphor for the darkness

Cruising in the Citadel Park takes place around the clock and in the open, but it is after dark that the park really comes to life (Hirsch, *Homotopia* 4).

The masking of darkness allows some of us the freedom to make love without masks, and for others the mask of anonymity serves the same purpose. I [Julius Fast] have had male homosexuals tell me that they have had encounters with men, complete from pickup to sexual satisfaction, without even divulging their own names or learning their partners' names. When I asked how they could be so intimate without ever knowing their partners' names, the answer was invariably: "But that adds something to it. I can be relaxed and do what I want to. After all, we didn't know each other, and who cares what we did or said?" (Fast 76)

The night intensifies the cover. It creates an atmosphere that draws a man out of his daily life. The night, along with the park, signifies a double anonymity. That anonymity for some makes for an extra sexual stimulator.[4]

"In fact, walking in the Citadel Park is my dark side. I don't easily talk about that. Or no, maybe now I do. Previously, I would not do it, on no account. Now I can contextualise all those things," says a nightly gay visitor. In the Citadel Park his "activities" take place, but never in daylight. They need to be strictly private: "Actually, I don't go there often. . . only when I feel down or horny. But that horny mood quickly passes when I walk around there. Initially I want to talk to somebody. If he immediately takes off his trousers. . . " To the question whether these men consider the park an extension of their gardens (a sense which most straight people confirm) one gay man reacts with force: "That's a good one: the park as garden! No, I don't consider that as my garden at all. I would never want to live around the park. Then I would go in too often. It could become an addiction! There are men like that." This exclamation suggests that for gay men there are actually three worlds. There is the "public world," which is the "official world": the world of paid work amongst colleagues. Then there is the private world, that of the own dwelling. Finally, there is the "ultimate private-world" that lies not in the private home anymore, but again in the public realm. However, this last relies on the anonymity of the public space. There are overlaps between the significance of public and private. One of the most private needs is articulated and met in the public sphere.

"Location" and "Locale"

Dafna Hirsch, who did similar research on the Independence Park in Tel Aviv, distinguished the two same kinds of motivations for visiting the Park, as I found for the Citadel Park.

There are men who come to Independence Park in order to feel "homosexual" (one of the interviewees said he used to feel "at home" in the park; another one said it was the feeling of being in a queer space where he could "speak the language" which made the park so favourable to him, whereas he couldn't stand the noise and smother of the bars and clubs); and there are others who come there so as not to feel "homosexual," for the park, with its blurring of the demarcations between "insider" and "outsider," allows them to express, and sometimes to experience the (self) ambiguity of "the man walking his dog," riding his bicycle, or making "anthropological research" (Hirsch, *Tel Aviv* 66).

This distinction is articulated in Strauss's terms: *location* (Fr. place) and *locale* (Fr. location) (Oosterdam 69-71). *Location* or place refers to the isolation of parts of the public space, that are sometimes, only at specific times, the exclusive domain, the living room, of a specific social-cultural group. In the first part of this article, I described how that living room of queer desire is enacted. It becomes an "underworld," a "dark side." "*Locale*" or location indicates the public space that serves as stage for people from different socio-cultural backgrounds, as a place of confrontation and interaction between representatives from different socio-cultural backgrounds (Oosterman 69-71). It is thus important that the park is public, accessible for everybody. Public spaces are the corner-stone of the local gay scene (Duyves 74) because of their great accessibility. An interviewee says that he never enters gay bars, but that he has no problem walking into the park. "Cross contacts," i.e., contacts between different subgroups are rather limited in the Citadel Park. But that doesn't reduce the fact that the presence of other subgroups is much appreciated. It makes gays feel they are not easily supervised: they can be walking there just like "anybody else." The presence of others guarantees the ultimate privacy they need when they are cruising in public. An analysis of other subgroups is not within the scope of this paper. We will, however, take a look at a subgroup that makes use of the same spatial provisions as gay men do.

Norm-exceeding behaviour

Many interviewees, including gays, point out that in recent years feelings of unsafety have been abetted by an increase in crime. Newspapers depict the park as dangerous, with a high crime rate, including rape and blackmail. "In 2001 there were in the King Albert Park, the Citadel Park and the Baudeloo Park, respectively 33, 42 and 13 crimes committed, much more than the 4 at the Blaarmeersen, a big recreation park" (*De Standaard* Online 14/02/2002) There were arguably even more crimes in the Citadel Park, but many queers value anonymity too much to report crimes to the police (*Het Laatste Nieuws*, 27/05/1998). Now that the perpetrators have access to the informants' files, the reporting rate has decreased further. According to the police, the perpetrators are frequently drug addicts who threaten their victims with knifes or tear-gas.

According to a policeman of the Special Detective Division:

> Also other people, who don't mean well, come to these places. There is paid sex, there prostitution. Some men are blackmailed and in the worst cases they are robbed and knocked down. Recently, we have been seeing in Ghent increasingly gay battering. Groups of dysfunctional youths come from surrounding neighbourhoods to defy and thrash people. The neighbours are also hindered by that aggressive folk, which increases the feelings of insecurity. (cited in Libert 1999)

The park is not socially safe (an aspect that rightly stands high on the feminist agenda). The spatial organisation is no help in this respect. The hilly landscape is difficult to control and absolutely unsurveyable. The surveillance and involvedness by other park-visitors is almost null. The numerous paths and enclosures just help the delinquents to hide themselves. The aspects which make the park attractive for gay men, make it equally attractive for the offenders. Both groups use the same spatial provisions. They prefer a lot of anonymity and many hiding places. They both also prefer the night, the darkness. They appreciate the tortuous paths which make them hard to see from afar. The big number of entrances and good accessibility increase the attractiveness of the park for pickpockets, while the unwillingness of homosexual and bisexual men who come here looking for illicit diversion, to report crimes, makes them suitable victims.[5] But other subgroups, like women and seniors, are also potential victims. The relative absence of women in the park may be explained by the preponderance of crime. People develop strategies to secure their safety and those of their children. One of them is avoiding the park at night. All the women

I queried said they did just that, as did also senior citizens and even some gay men.

First step towards a design

Within the framework of my Masters thesis on urban planning, I went beyond the analytical phase and gave some recommendations about the development of the park. It is important, however, to keep in mind that a total design for the park must include elements other than social concerns, like its flora and fauna, its significance for the city, mobility, other functions of the park buildings, the urban structure plan, etc.

At first glance, the park functions very well for cruisers. The problem is social safety: it touches not just gay men but especially other subgroups such as women, children, and the elderly. That problem is not easily solved because there is an incongruity between the spatial needs of gays and those of other subgroups. That incongruity occurs in the appreciation of the hiding possibilities by gay men and the desire for a socially safe environment among the elderly, women and children, but also among the gay men themselves. The duality is to do, on the one hand, with an urge to adventure, desire, taking risks and the challenge of danger, and, on the other hand, with the need of safety. Can those opposite demands be reconciled? An equilibration and a complementation between both spheres is missing at the moment.

Therefore I argue for the layout of some easily surveyable, wide, and safe strips of lawn and flowers along the walking paths in the park. The south side of the park, which contains the big, surveyable lake, should acquire a more open character. It should become a very open and ultra safe zone, in which women and children can walk and play without any danger. Besides good connections within the park, the isolated park should itself be linked with its surroundings. Besides these safety and access-related measures, I recommend other safety measures in the north part of the park, which should at the same time preserve its mysterious sphere. The caves and the bushes are basic elements of the park and its history. Measures are needed to increase the surveyability of the park in a way that would preserve its hiding possibilities for cruisers; therefore, some strategic, specifically localized interventions are necessary. A few SOS-stations should be placed in strategic places in the hills, so that people (mostly gay men) who are in danger, can immediately call for help. In the building complex I recommend a catalyst facility for activating 'cross contacts.' Restaurants, a cyber café, a crèche, an exhibit space and other functions could make of the hall a tourist attraction.

In my recommendations I look for an equilibration between the needs for safety of subgroups like seniors, women and children on the one hand, and those of the cruising men on the other. The dense bushes, caves and the hills should remain, in spite of the limited safety they offer. They insure a public, democratic playground for queer desire nearby the city centre. Thus, while certain specific measures should be implemented to discourage criminals, the park must not be fully controlled, lest it lose a part of its identity. I would like to end with the controversial words from a gay man of thirty three: "That's specific to all parks. The [gay] scene is always there. Otherwise it isn't a park."

Illustrations

Fig. 1 Plan of the Citadel Park

Fig. 2 Music Kiosk

Fig. 3 "There is also the cave with the cascade."

Fig. 4 "A little path goes upstairs, and then you arrive between al those little bushes."

Out Here: Local and International Perspectives in Queer Studies 91

Fig. 5 Uphill

Fig. 6 "Also on top of the other, smaller cave—or no, it's more like an arch—something can be seen."

92 The Citadel Park

Fig. 7 Main cruising street

Fig. 8 "You want to meet people there."

Out Here: Local and International Perspectives in Queer Studies 93

Fig. 9 "But they mustn't see you."

Fig. 10 A big anonymity and lots of hiding possibilities.

Fig. 11 The more open part

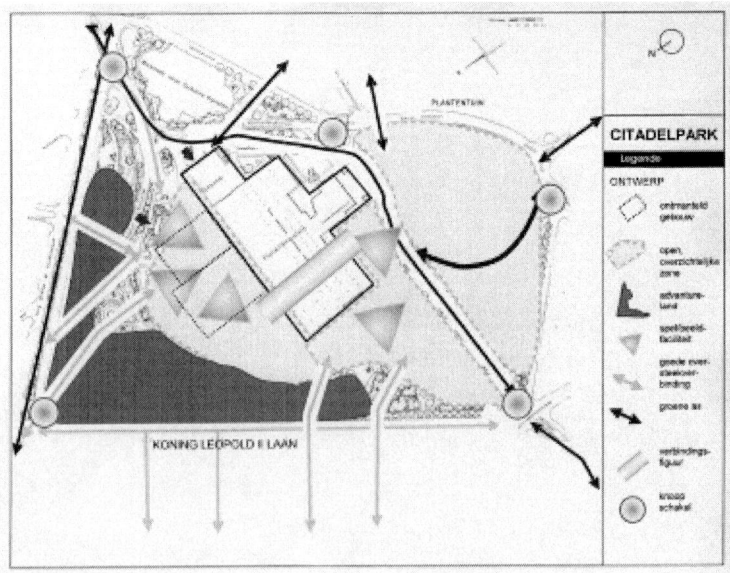

Fig. 12 Plan design proposal

Notes

1. The term "homosexual," as it is commonly used in Dutch, applies to man-man relations. The word "lesbian" is used explicitly for woman-woman relations. "Queers" is used for both groups. For the sake of simplicity, we classify homosexuals and bisexuals as "gays" or "men with a queer desire."
2. In Belgium the government introduced an equal opportunities policy in 1991. Initially that policy was only destined for (heterosexual) women. In 1995 it was widened to include gays and lesbians, people with disability, and foreigners. 1995 can by see as the year of birth of a strategic Flemish queer-policy. Earlier, queers supported the gay and lesbian initiatives (information elicited by the Belgian holebifederatie: info@fwh.be, 14 Mar. 2003).
3. By my own observations and the interviews. See also Hirsch (66): ". . . and a woman who enters is excluded from the park itself (an exclusion that is not only metaphorical—I could well feel it in my own body when I visited the park)." (translation of an unpublished paper) Fast (60) uses the term "non-person" to indicate that some people are "non-people" in a certain position for other people. For example: "The janitor who empties the waste basket in an office, may not bother to knock when he enters, nor does the occupant of the office mind this intrusion. The janitor is not a real person to him. He is a non-person just as the man in the office is a non-person to the janitor."
4. Els Maesschalck notes that the darkness generates a strong feeling of anonymity and a momentary character. She refers to the "one-night-stand" (180-181).
5. According to the coordinator of Social Issues in Ghent.

Works Cited

Betsky, Aaron. *Queer Space. Architecture and Same-Sex Desire.* New York: William Morrow and Company, Inc., 1997.

Chauncey, George, and D. A. Miller. "Outings." Joel Sanders *Stud. Architectures of Masculinity.* Ed. Princeton: Princeton architectural press, 1996. 223-277.

Deherdt, R., C. Deseyn, and W. Van Den Hole. *100 Jaar Plantsoenendienst—Promenades-Parken-Funktioneel groen.* Gent: Stad Gent, 1985. 59-70.

Duyves, Mattias. "In de ban van de bak. Openbaar ruimtegebruik naar homoseksuele voorkeur in Amsterdam." *De Uitstad. Over Stedelijk Vermaak.* Ed. Jack Burgers. Utrecht: Jan van Arkel, 1992. 73-97.

Fast, Julius. *Body Language.* New York: M. Evans and Company, 1970. (In Dutch: Fast, Julius, *De taal van het lichaam,* Utrecht: Servire Uitgevers, 1997.)

François, Philippe and Jef. Rosiers. "Vele slachtoffers stappen nooit naar politie." *Het Laatste Nieuws* 27 May 1998.

Hirsch, Dafna. "Tel-Aviv: rendez-vous à l'Independence Park." *Revue Urbanisme. Dossier: Corps et sexualités* 325 (2002): 64-66.

———. "Homotopia": Independence Park in Tel Aviv as Queer Space, s.d. 20 (extended, still unpublished version of previous article).

Libert, Marijke. "Het Gentse Citadelpark, Landschap en herinnering—Een park om langs te lopen." *De Morgen* 8 may 1999.

Maesschalck, Els. "Stedelijke Nacht." Master's Diss. University of Ghent, 1999.

Oosterman, Jan. "Kijken en bekeken worden. Over de opmars van het horeca terras." *De Uitstad. Over stedelijk vermaak*. Ed. Jack Burgers. Utrecht: Uitgeverij Jan van Arkel, 1992. 57-72.

Sioen, Peter. Het jongenskwartier—Straatprostitutie in Brussel. Antwerpen: Dedalus, 1996.

Van Gemert, Frank. "Fatale seks. Oorzaak en aanleiding van moorden met homoseksuele slachtoffers." *Het verlies van de Onschuld. Seksualiteit in Nederland*. Ed. Gert Hekma et al. Groningen: Wolters-Noordhoff, 1990. 169-192.

"Gent telt drie 'gevaarlijke' parken." *De standaard Online*, N.V. Vlaamse Uitgeversmaatschappij (VUM), 14 Febr. 2002 <http://www.destandaard.be>.

JUST POPPING?
ANTI-HOMOPHOBIC ELEMENTS IN SPANISH AND
CATALAN CONTEMPORARY POPULAR MUSIC[1]

ALFONS GREGORI I GOMIS

The Spanish generation which started their education after the fall of Franco's regime, in 1975, has grown up in an increasingly more open-minded and dynamic society. During the last twenty five years, contemporary popular music has been developing its areas of pop and rock, leaving behind a long period of obscurantism that accepted only quiet and sugary manifestations of these musical styles. The young-oriented cultural movements wanted to move beyond the politically engaged and melodically monotonous protest song, to discover a new world of beats beyond the gray concrete of the expanding Spanish cities. One of the subjects that became a focus of interest for some left-wing pop or rock bands and singers was sexuality, mainly heterosexual, treated at first as a new hedonistic experience. Only after a slow process, a few gay messages came out from the heterosexist closet where they had previously remained. Quite naturally, this was not easy, and still a great deal of clearly homophobic or masculinist lyrics can be found among rock and pop records, even in works of several supposedly progressive authors. The Spanish and Western phallogocentrism implied that lesbian and queer representations in lyrics came up in the mass-media only after a public embodiment of male homosexuality was achieved.

In an interesting short article about politics on (homo)sexuality in Spain, Kerman Calvo claims that Spanish society was not ready to understand gay and lesbian demands during the 1980s (182). This situation involved the weak status of gay and lesbian organizations in relation to the contemporary political parties and institutions. However, it must be taken into account that, thanks to the first socialist government in this decade, Spanish public opinion became more tolerant to ideas or images that some years before would have been simply unthinkable. But the regressive and homophobic institutional politics of Margaret Thatcher and Ronald Reagan (Fernàndez 16-17) did not promote a positive perception of homosexuality in Spain, a country more and more receptive to modernization, where the cultures of both North America and Great Britain served as points of reference. In the English-speaking world a revolt against homophobic cultural politics was personified and carried out by techno-pop bands like Frankie Goes to Hollywood, Bronski Beat or Culture Club, which offered a most explicit gay aesthetics.

The objective of this article is to analyze a selected group of lyrics, sung in Spanish or Catalan[2] from the beginning of the 1980s until the end of the 1990s, in order to explain the strategies and positions of gay, lesbian and queer sexual orientations used by musicians, in relation both to certain theories of gender and popular music that focus on the notions of authenticity and artifice, and to multidisciplinary works on gender politics. The songs' classification in this article will follow the categories "lesbian," "gay" and "transgender" usually encountered in academic works, while pointing out their historically contingent condition and their status as "a necessary error," that Gayatri Chakravorty Spivak would define as catachrestic (Butler, "Imitation" 16). As an outstanding case among the rest of the discussed bands, we will attentively consider that of Mecano, the most important representatives of pop music in Spain during the two aforementioned decades. At the same time, we will avoid the use of unknown songs or bands, selecting only those sufficiently popularized through mass-media, that is to say television, radio or, at the moment, the Internet, to be easily recognizable at least in their time. As our work aims at discussing the sexual politics and morality of the whole society, we must assume that any rarely available lyrics were at best an isolated, if disruptive, voice.[3]

1. Mecano's "Sólo soy una persona": the first outcry

From our point of view, the song "Sólo soy una persona," from the LP record *Mecano* (1982), should be considered the first song for the mass audience trying to break the stereotyped conventions about homosexuality in the newly born democracy. Mecano, the band which dominated the Spanish pop scene until the end of the 1990s, has been accused, explicitly or implicitly, of playing only for commercial reasons. Nevertheless, the band composed a few intelligent and unconventional songs that allowed thousands of young people to rethink their sexuality beyond the old heterosexual categories. "Sólo soy una persona" exemplifies this claim, although it fails to offer a coherent theoretical ground linking its humanist ideals and the notion of gendered otherness. The monologue of the lyrical I is built upon two foundations: the denial of any heterosexual categorization ("*I am neither a man nor a woman*") in the chorus, and, in the remaining part of the lyrics, a continuous negative self-definition as a human being that avoids any kind of artistic objectification.

The body of the lyrical I remains a *tabula rasa* which leads to a complete lack of the subject's gendering. While attempting to avoid homophobic attitudes, this gender emptiness seems to offer the phallogocentric entity that liberal pseudo-humanism calls the "Human being." Nevertheless, the value of the song lies in its radical assumption of Monique Wittig's postulates: "The refusal to become (or to remain) heterosexual always meant to refuse to become a man or a woman, consciously or not" (13). Mecano's discourse attacks the ontological conception that differentiates "man-being" and "woman-being," considering them a politically operative binary inscribed in the heterosexual system, as Wittig does (29). Even though "Sólo soy una persona" is but an outcry, it betrays its authors'desire to transform the oppressing reality of contemporary Spanish mentality.

2. "Mujer contra mujer": a lesbian hit

"Mujer contra mujer," (Woman against woman) from the LP record *Descanso dominical* of Mecano, is the most popular song dedicated to lesbian love in Spain. Quite unexpectedly, this song succeeded in the pop-music market, becoming the number one hit not only in Spain, but also in France when rerecorded with French lyrics. The theoretical references of this song were radically different from the previous example. The very title points to a categorization of two lesbians as "women," whereas the materialist feminist Wittig concludes her astonishing article "The Straight Mind" (first published in 1980) as follows: "It would be incorrect to say that lesbians associate, make love, live with women, for 'woman' has meaning only in heterosexual systems of thought and heterosexual economic systems. Lesbians are not women" (32). The subverting elimination of gender from "Sólo soy una persona" has been substituted by a reinforced feminization of the main characters in "Mujer contra mujer." Another interesting point of this song is the use of the word "contra," corresponding to the English preposition "against."This usage plays with the ambiguity of two meanings: the negative one of "opposition" and the positive one of "contact." The ambiguity persists in the lyrics, which on the one hand evoke a shadowy zone linked, by the first meaning, to the heterosexual society, while on the other, the second meaning points to another zone, where lesbian love can be freely articulated.

The song is constructed upon the axis of dichotomized spaces, setting an invisible border between the two protagonists and the world of compulsory heterosexuality. The lesbians go as far as to build a metaphorical wall made of stones taken from the heap which symbolically represents innocence, a reference to the Jews who wanted to stone to death a sexually "deviant"[4] person: the adulteress from the Gospel according to Saint John (8, 2-12). Private space functions as the only place of real communication between the lovers, objectified in the imperceptible darkness under the tablecloth, in contrast to the public heterosexual space. In this specific frame, lesbians hide themselves in anonymity, given that the lyrical I calls them "one" and "the other." In Teresa de Lauretis's terms, major political failure lies in the sole use of a mask, or in living in secretive isolation, instead of setting the scene with a complete masquerade. However, the most elaborated dichotomy of spaces in "Mujer contra mujer" is symbolized by the low flight of two doves out of reach of any radar, representing lesbian freedom. The subtext is that the radar not only means a control weapon, but it also drives the birds to mechanization, to act like planes. Consequently, technology becomes a tool of heterosexual social oppression.

The embryo-like power of the woman-identified women is absolutely absent from Mecano's lyrics, which has no liberationist function. To feminize the love scenes by means of Luce Irigaray's metaphorical constructs of "solidary" embracing lips as textually symbolic counter-representation of male phallus falls into the aestheticism of difference, such as that of the Italian group *Libreria delle Donne-Milano* and Luisa Muraro. The concept of women as doves furnishes further arguments about this analogy, because of the connotations of peace, opposed to the essentially aggressive and warlike patriarchal structures. This conservative and seprationist vision diminishes any possibility of lesbian politics, or a release from the heterosexual matrix.

3. Gay songs: irony and technology undermining the straight way

Los Burros's "Mi novia se llamaba Ramón," (My fiancée's name is Ramon) from the LP record *Rebuznos de amor* (1983), was one of the first truly interesting songs explicitly speaking about a male homosexual relationship. The record's title, meaning "brays of love," reflects the irony overflowing most of its lyrics. The song's title splices a feminine category and a masculine first name. The textual frame of the lyrics subverts the traditional coherence, built by men in power by means of patriarchal institutions. The irony of the song, far from denigrating homosexuality as a social or psychological deformity, dismantles the mechanisms of discrimination implemented by Western society in order to keep homosexuality on the margins. Moreover, this irony creates a renewed network of relations between signs of gender and of mourning. In the lyrics there even appears a joke about the words ending in *-on*, like Ramón, the name of the dead lover, which implicitly refers to *maricón*, a Spanish word of abuse meaning "queer"; or the morbidly ridiculous circumstances of his/her death in an accident with a lorry, crowned by a funny description of the skull bouncing on the highway.

The use of humor starts a sympathetic process connecting the lyrical I and the listener. The love story shows an unlikely normality, that is to say, the gay couple carry out all the mundane actions of a heterosexual couple (they go dancing and take a stroll), engaging in public display of tender acts, like kissing. Humor and tenderness help to gender in another way a world with normal gay relationships. Freedom of sexual orientation becomes the key to the song, which deconstructs the body of Ramón by limiting the importance of physical difference in sexuality. In this sense, the body not only reflects a determinate socioeconomic structure, but it is the tool for a change of perspective on homosexuality.

In 1989, the first Catalan LP (*Ho sento molt*) from the singer Albert Pla, who afterwards recorded some of his works in Spanish, was released in Catalonia. Pla includedon this record two interesting songs with male homosexual motifs: "La nana de l'Antonio" and "La violació." In the first one, the lyrical I explains, in a very ironical tone, reactions to and the consequences of the death of Antonio, a pimp to sixteen prostitutes, who is called *marica*, a word equivalent to "queer." Antonio is nasty but ambiguous from the ethical point of view: he gave away coats to old exhibitionists and offered drugs to children, while he also sponsored reading among youth like a modern gay Robin Hood. As a result of his death, Ernest, a sixteen-year-old homosexual, commits suicide, motivated by passion. Antonio, the personification of the worst vice, acquires in this lullaby a strongly sympathetic nature in a way that persuades the listener of the irrelevance of certain dichotomized ways of seeing things: homosexuality is the middle ground in the song, situated between the exploitation of prostitutes and the sponsoring of readership among the young; it is also presented as a combination of love and sex.

The second song from this record tells the story of a male rape committed by a "big" man and three women. We find once again the satirical attitude characterizing Pla's artistic work. In comparison with "La nana de l'Antonio," however, "La violació" contains an even more complicated textual game of male homosexual representation. The weaker sex of women is subverted by the description of the female characters' aggressiveness, which permits the collective rape. The lyrical I, the victim, uses numerous adjectives to describe the effects of the attack on his body. The majority of them emphasize the violence suffered, but a remarkable number could be considered a homophobic response to the male aggressor: *enculat* (ass-penetrated), *ultratjat* (outraged), *deshonrat* (dishonored) or *rebaixat* (humiliated). These words appear in combination with other adjectives to point up how pure violence is a way (not only for a man) to obtain pleasure. However, the song refers neither to a heterosexual rape (the only object of erotic interest for the aggressors is the victim's anus) nor to the rapist's member or the phallic instruments used to penetrate the body. Another remarkable aspect is the setting because, quite ironically, the rape takes place in a wood. The situation is therefore similar to that of the popular fairy-tale *The Little Red Riding Hood*, which can be read as warning against the consequences of an innocent little girl's intrusion into the male dominion. All these elements suggest some sort of womanly ritual for taking revenge on male patriarchal power, with the women empowering themselves by means of a raping man whom they use as a tool. In this sense, the victim's homophobia would be the reinforcement of heterosexual men's traditional attitudes towards "Otherness": panic and hate conveyed through a language that sets hierarchies among sexed bodies.

The Catalan band Els Pets released the song "Perdut al mig del Sitges" (*Els Pets*) in the same year. In stark contrast to the previous author's style, Els Pets's song works simply as entertainment using some homophobic stereotypes. (Situated on the seashore in the south of Barcelona, Sitges is considered the Catalan gay capital, especially during the summer holidays.) The band's next LP, *Calla i balla* (1991), includes "S'ha acabat," an elaborated and subtle song about the reactions and memories of a young man left by his boyfriend. This song could be seen as an act of contrition for "Perdut al mig de Sitges" ("Lost in the middle of Sitges"). The virtues of the song lie in the presentation of the couple's love both in the public sphere (the beach) and in a private space (the boyfriend's flat), while the song's form of an intimate monologue "normalizes" and makes understandable the subject's feelings. However, its anti-homophobic power is lessened by the manner in which the actual sexual orientation of the lovers is eventually disclosed: it canonly be glimpsed when the lyrical I mentions the arrival on the scene of a girl who disappears with his boyfriend.

In "Stereosexual," a song from Mecano's last LP *Ana/Jose/Nacho* (1998), male homosexuality becomes something "presumed." Its lyrical I, a life-long straight man suffering from a devastating hangover, thinks that he had sex with another man. At the end of the song, however, he finds out that his partner is a woman with short hair. This song leaves aside most of the platitudes about gay promiscuity and destabilizes gender by calling into question the very idea of sexual orientation as a corner-stone of identity. Certainly, the lyrical I has doubts about his having become bisexual because of a single sexual act with another man, labeling this possibility with the technological notion of "stereosexuality." Therefore, gendering is typified as a technology, abandoning the hypothesis about a sexual identity subjected to biology. As Teresa de Lauretis and Donna Haraway have remarked, gender is a technology[5] that obscures the mechanisms by which gender is rendered natural (Halberstam 186). Moreover, Butler's definition of gender[6] conceptualizes its production by looking to the quantity of the gendering acts, not merely to their quality. In "Stereosexual," the subject fears his own performative turning into someone "half-gay," finally deciding to go on with his previous heterosexual orientation. However, the very possibility of choice, granted by cultural elements such as technology, offers a really productive new point of view on homosexuality.

4. Transgenders[7] revolt: the last failed step?

In 1987, the composer and singer Victor Manuel released his LP record *Qué te puedo dar*, including the song "Como los monos de Gibraltar." The title of the song evokes the Gibraltar monkeys, known in Spain for their habit of shading their eyes with one of their paws. Its protagonist is Gaspar, a young transsexual[8] from a very traditionalist family of military patriarchs, that is: the monkeys.[9] Nevertheless, thanks to some family arrangements with bureaucracy, he manages to regulate his new social identity after his sex change. Gaspar breaks the conventional sex-gender causality but otherwise he opts for the heterosexual rules: he even studies to become an officer of the army. According to Judith Butler's assumption of Esther Newton's theories, drag implies that any gendering is an impersonation and approximation, one which, moreover, enacts heterosexual *pathos*: the impossibility of reaching the "perfect" gender original ("Imitation" 20-21, 31). However, Víctor Manuel's song lacks the subversive function that Butler ascribes to some gay imitations of the traditional gendering because the character Gaspar renounces any transgression of the heterosexual norm beyond his-her change of sex ("Imitation" 22-23). As Esther Núñez (134) affirms, the medical articulation of transsexuality gives to gender dissidents an existential meaning against their suffering. The passage where Gaspar is "taken by the waist" (as the song expresses it) symbolizes perfectly his-her subjection to the phallocentric norms.

Tam Tam Go's "Manuel-Raquel" is the Spanish language version of the song "Lawrence's Heart is Weak," from *Spanish Shuffle* (1988), the first LP of this initially English-singing band entitled. Manuel-Raquel is an abnormally composed name because its first part is masculine and the second feminine. The reason is the presumed double nature of Manuel-Raquel as a drag queen, embodied in a man while having a feminine mind. His-her suicidal end is provoked by his-her desperation and helplessness in an intolerant society. Even though the lyrical I shows sympathy towards the character, his-her suicide implies a homophobic view of he character's supposedly womanly (cowardly and hysterical) attitude toward existence. The same attitude is exemplified in the last chorus, which gives him-her a gentle characterization. The appearance of police, the armed hand of the phallogocentric power, and the radical change of name (from *Manuel* to *Raquel*) register his-her possible occupation as prostitute. That is why he-she can be located on the margins of the heterosexual matrix, which the lyrical I blames for his-her death. In looking at the sexual inversion commonplace: *anima mulieris in corpore virile inclusa*, "Como los monos de Gibraltar" and "Manuel-Raquel" mark the (failed) extremes of drag: from complete reintegration in the patriarchal grid, combined with effacing any mark of rebellion, to that grid's absolute refusal—in self-annihilation.

Among their numerous classically heterosexual songs, the Catalan pop band Sau also wrote one dealing with drag behavior: "Sense estil" ("Without style") (*No puc deixar de fumar*, 1989). The essentialism that characterizes Sau appears again in the inversion trope mentioned above: "You will reflect so subtly, from the very inside, your femininity." Certainly, the title of the song indicates drag's incapacity to manage or perform troublesome identities. At its end, the song seems to allude to the Pet Shop Boys' "It's a sin." According to Stan Hawkins: "By disrupting stereotypical codes of gender and sexuality through a parody of artifice and masquerade that challenges patriarchy, these artists remind us that music can function as a key vehicle in deconstructing fixed notions of gendered identity in every day life" (118). However, the Catalan musicians do not attempt to celebrate the sexual disruptions offered by the Pet Shop Boys. Even drag is not always a subversive activity, as Butler argues (*Bodies* 231).

We discover an attitude quite contrary to that in Sau's song in Albert Pla's Spanish language version of Lou Reed's "Walk On the Wild Side," a single hit included on his LP *Pla supone Fonollosa* (1995). Pla's song is not a literal translation, though it reproduces the main statements about each of the characters of Reed's lyrics, adopting suitable Spanish circumstances and names that contribute to a rich performative irony. In this case, Holly, the drag personage that opens the English original, is bifurcated into a masculine *Manolo* and a feminine *Manoli*. Besides the fact that *Manolo* is *per se* a name with pejorative connotations, in Pla's lyrics it subtly but effectively evokes the Spanish actress Bibi Andersen, who played several roles in Pedro Almodóvar's films. Andersen was very popular in Spain during the 1980s because he-she became one of the first notorious transsexual artists. Before this notoriety he-she was Manolo Fernández. Appropriating Reed's work for the Spanish conditions, Pla adapts the critical, grave and urbane tone of the New York artist to the local imaginary and introduces new subversive elements like drag, displacing his discourse as far or further than Reed towards a constructionist vision of sexuality.

5. Just popping?

In these concluding lines, we should start from focusing our attention on a general frame connecting contemporary popular music and (homo)sexuality. Norma Coates adopts the concept of gender as technology and she applies it to rock music, taking into account the discursive and stylistic segregation of "rock" and "pop" that identifies the former with authenticity and masculinity, and the latter with artificiality and femininity. Coates's statements such as "real men aren't pop, and women, real or otherwise, don't rock" or "'pop' music is allegedly sick, prefabricated ... and other 'feminine' or 'feminized' recreations" explain graphically the homophobic tendencies inside the rock's aesthetic and ethical network, facilitating the confinement of anti-homophobic tendencies into pop-music production (52-53). The importance of irony and new technologies in some of the discussed songs, as a way of implementing a different paradigm towards male homosexual orientations, reminds us of the capacity of the British Pet Shop Boys[10] to shift the position of masculinity through strategies such as irony or defiance (Hawkins 118). Unfortunately, neither Spanish nor Catalan cultures have enjoyed a local pop band similar either in the incisiveness of its lyrics or in massive popularity.

On the one hand, the word "pop" used in the title of the present article means a musical and cultural style or attitude, on the other, it refers to the sound of opening a bottle, a sound that may metonymically connote an ephemeral and (at last) frustrating condition.The analysed songs' status as popular hits allows performative effects against homophobia, pursued by most of the lyrical I's. However, according to Butler:

> If a performative provisionally succeeds..., then it is not because an intention successfully governs the action of speech, but only because that action echoes prior actions, and *accumulates the force of authority through the repetition or citation of a prior, authoritative practices*.... In this sense, no term or statement can function performatively without the accumulating and dissimulating historicity of force. (*Bodies* 226-227)

Consequently, must not our frustration with the limited political efficacy of those songs originate in the very status of pop music as an ephemeral entity incapable of leaving enough traces to establish an "historicity of force"? It may be that the central problem to discuss is the actual function of the pop-music canon, from the national and international point of view.[11] Besides, the constructionist perspective, used throughout this paper for commenting on the songs, has been charged with depoliticizing theory (Fernàndez 21) because it questions the presentist assumptions in contemporary identity categories (Butler, *Bodies* 227). Yet, if identities make possible and produce social collectives, moral links, and political agency (Seidman 101), what is the function of pop songs in relation to that? Is it just "popping" like a bottle of red, red wine, or is it "popping" as a *continuum* of gender displacements that work against fixed identity categories?

We should consider here both the very contingency of identities (undergoing nonetheless a process of congealing over time) and the notion of authenticity previously brought up in relation to sexuality in contemporary popular music. The effectiveness of the performative act depends in a non-negligible measure on the performer's status and presence, represented through his/her empowered capacity for convicing. Authenticity is that which prompts us to take the lyrics seriously, and in this sense it is one of the factors working for the success of performative art. If pop music is popularly perceived as lacking in authenticity, then the political message of the texts could not performatively communicate anti-homophobic attitudes to the listeners. However, the characterization of identity offered below, which renders suspect both its supposed essentialist stability and its permanent fluidity, provides a contingent solution to this problem: non-authenticity allies with non-identity, producing a potential for the subversion of homophobia. As Lawrence Grossberg (202) argues, pop music "becomes a self-conscious parody of the ideology of authenticity, by making the artificiality of its construction less a matter of aesthetics and more a matter of image-marketing." On these terms, pop music may disclose the constructed condition of the processes of both authenticity and gendering, by means of the same mechanisms of suspicion: "The only possible claim to authenticity is derived from the knowledge and admission of your inauthenticity" (Grossberg 206). The key which consolidates this alliance is irony, which breaks the pact of authenticity by imposing its own norms on trusting the possible message of the lyrics.

In any case, our explanation of anti-homophobic elements in the reviewed Spanish and Catalan songs must combine the effects of a society not yet ready to accept homosexuality, a set of pro-gay organizations unable to cope with this situation, and a relatively weak reflection of these phenomena by the music market. This combination of circumstances leaves little space for a materialization of the postulated alliance, all the more so given Butler's point that judgments about what is really subversive are useless because "they cannot be made in ways that endure through time" (*Gender* xxi). Consequently, the fragility of pop resides in the very core of subversiveness. One hopes that songs like "Mujer contra mujer" or "Stereosexual," in spite of their problems of conceptualization, may lay the seeds for a new generation of bands, like Ellos or Astrud. In relation to this organic allegory of the textual function in modern music, Steven Seidman (70) champions a notion of postmodernism constituted by local, multiple and linked struggles to create social spaces where some forms of individuation and democratization are able to proliferate. This should be the aim of future bands, trying to exorcise the homophobic views of the Spanish and Catalan culture and society by means of a more effective performative activity, in an ever dynamic reformulation of gendering. Nevertheless, if the set of subversive gestures contained in the analyzed lyrics (seen as reflecting an anti-identity or post-identity position) lacks the coherence posited by Seidman (102), then the very notion of popular music loses any social function and is condemned to the most useless banality.

Notes

1. I would like to dedicate this article to my friends Alba and Marga. I especially thank Krzysztof Fordoński and the editors for their patient correcting of the text.
2. The choice of these two languages is neither arbitrary nor subjective, as Spanish is the official language in the whole state while Catalan is the second most popular language in Spain. It is also the official language in Catalonia, Valencia and the Balearic Islands. However, the boom in pop and rock Catalan music took place late, at the end of the 1980s.
3. Similarly, we will not analyze the role of young pop bands like Ellos or Astrud, still well outside the mainstream, which present an openly gay attitude. However, they form an interesting current, performing their discourse between the limits of a contradictory camp aesthetics and a troublesome search for self-identity. Ellos, a band from Madrid, recently released its first LP record *Lo tuyo no tiene nombre* (2001), while Astrud, a more experimental duet from Barcelona, has two LP records on the market, *Mi fracaso personal* (1999) and *Gran fuerza* (2001).
4. We use this term not in a descriptive sense, but as an example of discrimination in linguistic commonplaces. It has been taken from Sigmund Freud, who considered "deviation" to be the sexual orientations or practices that strayed from heterosexuality, in other words, sexual "inversions" (homosexuality) or "perversions" (non-procreative sexual practices; Fernàndez 18).
5. "De Lauretis appropriates the Foucauldian term "technology," describing the way that power works productively to replicate and multiply itself, in order to explain how gendered social and cultural relations are reiterated and reinforced" (Coates 52).
6. "Gender is the repeated stylization of the body, a set of repeated acts within a highly rigid regularity frame that congeal over time to produce the appearance of substance, of a natural sort of being." (Butler, *Gender* 43-44)
7. This term is used in its most general meaning, that is to say, as referring to individuals who can not be represented within the dominant gender schemes. It includes transsexuals, transgenders stricto sensu (persons identified with no determinate normative gender identity, freely fluctuating between them), transvestites, drags or gender benders (Núñez 136).
8. It is interesting to observe the coincidence between the policeman's statement included in the lyrics, clarifying that Gaspar is not a social danger or problem, and the sociological discourse, for which transsexuality is not a social problem but a social question (Núñez 127).
9. Coming from the radically antimilitarist position of the generation that created the chanson against Franco, Víctor Manuel has always shown a very strong opposition to any sort of conservative attitude or ideology, especially in relation to the army.
10. However, in his book *Queer Noises* "[John] Gill also suggests that the Pet Shop Boys represent a new type of post-Thatcher conservatism through the compromising stance they take with respect to their sexuality" (Hawkins 126).

11. In this sense, the canon of Catalan contemporary popular music is substantially different from the Spanish one, because the songs in Catalan included in the present work may belong to the former, but none belongs to the latter, in spite of "sharing" bilingual songwriters like Albert Pla.

Works Cited

Butler, Judith. *Gender Trouble: Feminism and the Subversion of Identity.* New York and London: 1990; reprinted in Judith Butler. *Gender Trouble: Feminism and the Subversion of Identity.* 10th Anniversary Ed. New York and London: Routledge, 1999.

———. "Imitation and Gender Insubordination." *Inside/Out: Lesbian Theories, Gay Theories.* Ed. Diana Fuss. New York and London: Routledge, 1991; translated in *El gai saber: Introducció als estudis gais i lèsbics.* Ed. Josep-Anton Fernàndez. Barcelona: Llibres de l'Índex, 2000. 113-135.

———. *Bodies That Matter: On the Discursive Limits of "Sex."* New York and London: Routledge, 1993.

Calvo, Kerman. "Polítiques d'(homo)sexualitat a Espanya: Les respostes de la democràcia davant d'un dilema moral." *Sociologia de la sexualitat: Una aproximació a la diversitat sexual.* Ed. Òscar Guasch i Andreu. Barcelona: Pòrtic, 2002. 165-187.

Coates, Norma. "(R)Evolution Now?: Rock and the Political Potential of Gender." *Sexing the Groove: Popular Music and Gender.* Ed. Sheila Whiteley. London and New York: Routledge, 1997. 50-64.

Fernàndez, Josep-Anton. "Introducció." *El gai saber: Introducció als estudis gais i lèsbics.* Ed. Josep-Anton Fernàndez. Barcelona: Llibres de l'Índex, 2000. 11-29.

Grossberg, Lawrence. "The Media Economy of Rock Culture: Cinema, Postmodernity and Authenticity." *Sound and Vision: The Music Video Reader.* Eds. Simon Frith, Andrew Goodwin and Lawrence Grossberg. London: Routledge, 1993. 185-209.

Halberstam, Judith. "Techno-Homo: On Bathrooms, Butches, and Sex with Furniture." *Processed Lives: Gender and Technology in Everyday Life.* Eds. Jennifer Terry and Melodie Calvert. London and New York: Routledge, 1997. 183-193.

Hawkins, Stan. "The Pet Shop Boys: Musicology, Masculinity and Banality." *Sexing the Groove: Popular Music and Gender.* Ed. Sheila Whiteley. London and New York: Routledge, 1997. 118-133.

Lauretis, Teresa de. *Feminist studies / Critical studies.* Bloomington: Indiana University Press, 1986.

Núñez, Esther. "Transsexualisme, transgenerisme i sistemes de gènere." *Sociologia de la sexualitat: Una aproximació a la diversitat sexual.* Ed. Òscar Guasch i Andreu. Barcelona: Pòrtic, 2002. 123-139.

Seidman, Steven. "Identity and Politics in a 'Postmodern' Gay Culture: Some Historical and Conceptual Notes." *Fear of a Queer Planet: Queer Politics and Social Theory.* Ed. Michael Warner. Minneapolis and London: University of Minnesota Press, 1993; translated in *El gai saber: Introducció als estudis gais i lèsbics.* Ed. Josep-Anton Fernàndez. Barcelona: Llibres de l'Índex, 2000. 69-112.

Wittig, Monique. *The Straight Mind and Other Essays.* Boston: Beacon Press, 1992.

CHRIS BELL

ALL THE MEN ARE WHITE, LOOKS LIKE THE WOMEN ARE TOO, BUT SOME OF US KNOW BETTER

> I am an invisible man. . . . I am invisible, understand, simply because people refuse to see me."
>
> Ralph Ellison

> Sometimes, I feel discriminated against, but it does not make me angry. It merely astonishes me. How can any deny themselves the pleasure of my company? It's beyond me.
>
> Zora Neale Hurston

Introduction

I have heard it suggested that the most segregated time of the week in the United States is Sunday morning when churchgoers begin their worship. According to these observers, black individuals proceed to their churches of choice while white individuals head off to their religious comfort zones. Latinos, Asian-Americans and other racial and ethnic groups have staked their respective places as well. As if by design, intermingling is rare.

I would like to appropriate this observation because I think it is applicable to the queer community. In my estimation, the most segregated time of the week in the queer community is Friday/Saturday night when the masses head out to the bars. Enter virtually any queer bar in the U.S. and all you see is people of one race. This might seem a curious, perhaps specious, place to begin my paper, but let's not forget the queer community is the only one with the dubious distinction of beginning its modern-day push for civil rights in a bar.

With this in mind, I have chosen to unpack the conference theme a little differently from some of my fellow presenters. Instead of discussing discrimination and marginalization as they are leveled *against* queer folks, my intent is to examine those same tenets *within* the queer community. My principal focus therefore is discrimination based on the social construct of race. Although this paper is being presented in Poland where racism may not be as much of a conundrum as in other locales, the focal point is the U.S. because that is where I have lived for all twenty-eight years of my life. It is my hope this paper will illuminate the diverse, cosmopolitan nature of queer culture and community in the U.S., simultaneously calling into question the white-washed representation too many of us are familiar (read: inundated) with.

The Problem of the Color Line

Allow me to describe a typical night out at the bars in Chicago, the city I call home. When I enter a queer bar and see nothing but white men gathered, conventional wisdom posits that I am supposed to accept this without remark. I have always thought that if the average white dude entered a gay bar on the Halsted Strip in Chicago, Santa Monica Boulevard in West Hollywood, or Christopher Street in New York's Greenwich Village (all legendary queer locales) and saw nothing but black men gathered there, he would freak out and probably never return. The space that has been created in most queer bars across the U.S. is a space marketed to and patronized by white men. There is very little consideration given to racial and ethnic diversity within this aspect of the queer community. Instead, it's the same golden boys in attendance night after night, drink after drink.

Not so long ago, I had a conversation with an individual who suggested I address the fact that there are relatively few non-white patrons at Sidetrack, arguably the most popular queer bar in Chicago. This individual advised me to speak with the bar owner about the lack of diversity at his establishment. "He'll be receptive to your concerns," he assured me. I nodded sagely, and walked away fuming. Why should it be contingent on me to tell the bar owner something that is obvious? This person has eyes. He can see his establishment is not representative of the overarching queer community in Chicago. Evidently, he is not looking, unconcerned, or a combination of the two.

Moreover, I think it's interesting that a vast majority of Sidetrack's patrons spend hours in tanning booths, soaking up ultraviolet rays at abhorrent rates—coming close to contracting skin cancer—just so they can look like me, but they will not speak to me. I have lost track of how many times I have stood in that bar, ready and willing to engage in conversation with my queer "brothers," only to be ignored. This situation is reminiscent of a sentiment Maya Angelou conveys in her autobiographical novel *The Heart of a Woman*. While attending an elite party at New York's Waldorf-Astoria hotel, Angelou is

> ignored primarily because she is a black woman. She writes:I had a fresh haircut and was wearing the prettiest outfit I owned. I could speak French and Spanish very well and could talk intelligently on a number of subjects. I knew national politics intimately and international subjects moderately well. . . . Yet, no one talked to me. I had another drink. (238)

If I had a drink for every queer white man who shunned me because of my race, I can assure you I would drop dead from alcohol poisoning. Having said that, I do not think I am being overly-sensitive. Perhaps these queer white men are not attracted to, or are intimidated by, a cute young chocolate niblet such as myself. But they could at least say "Hello" or do something to acknowledge my presence. That's not so much to ask.

It is not, to clarify, just the race of the individuals who patronize the space that is problematic. In the four years I have sporadically ventured to Sidetrack, I have seen only one person of color working behind the bar. This of course places me in the delicate position of choosing to support my "brutha" or spreading out in a valiant attempt to integrate the bar. The reality isn't much different at other venues on the Halsted Strip. There's only one or two persons of color working at these bars. This dearth of racial and ethnic diversity is an inexcusable fact of life within the queer community. White queers conveniently tend to forget that the Stonewall patrons on that fateful evening in June 1969 were primarily black and Puerto Rican; thus, the lack of diversity in bar culture's present incarnation is all the more galling.

Additionally, the community events at some bars are not exactly troped with racial and ethnic diversity in mind. One of the more insensitive s(l)ights I have ever noted is one I observed earlier this summer while walking past a queer bar on the Halsted Strip. Prominently posted on the bar's marquee was the following: "Tonight: 7th Annual Slave Auction!!!" A slave auction. An event in which men stand on a stage in loincloth ensembles (or lesser garb in some instances) while the audience members ogle them and call out bids. After the "slaves" are "sold," they are expected to go home with their new "owners" for a predetermined amount of time to carry out their "master's" requests. One would imagine the organizers of this event would understand the phrase "slave auction" has a history, an undeniably pejorative denotation, for a significant segment of the queer community. One would hope the organizers would realize that it was not that long ago that the ancestors of black queers were bought, sold, and stolen from the African continent, brought to the U.S., and subsequently bartered in *bonafide* slave auctions. Apparently, no one had the foresight to bring this to the organizers' attention since it was, to emphasize, the seventh iteration of this event. I cannot imagine walking down Halsted Street and coming across a sign advertising a "Concentration Camp Auction." Imagine the proceedings: The participants (175 of them to commemorate Paragraph 175) are marched onto the stage single-file, ordered to strip, shave their heads, and stand under shower heads while the audience members taunt them. Perhaps the theme could be "Work Makes You Free?" No one would ever dream of doing this, but it is perfectly acceptable to have a slave auction. Egregious.

(I must pause here to acknowledge that I am fully aware of where I am standing as I read this paper. I know the concentration camps are nearby, and I know some audience members might have an inextricable link to these camps. For this reason, I apologize to anyone I may have offended with the previous example. I would ask the audience to bear in mind that the pain you may feel is similar to the sensation I felt upon viewing the "Slave Auction" marquee.)

* * *

The lack of racial and ethnic diversity in queer bars is representative of a larger dilemma within Chicago's queer community. Chicago is a city of 77 neighborhoods. This assessment excludes the city's suburbs and collar counties, but it is a fairly apt one to utilize when discussing the city proper. Chicago's queer neighborhood is in Lakeview, on the north side of the city. Many Chicagoans call this area "Boystown" in honor of the neighborhood's queer appeal. The mayor of Chicago has even erected a series of phallic rainbow pylons along Halsted Street in commemoration of the "special character" of Boystown. Clearly, queer Chicagoans have, to borrow a phrase from Virginia Woolf, a space of our own.

One point of contention I have with the designation of Boystown as the city's queer mecca is that it automatically discounts those queers who live in other areas of the city. For instance, there is a sizeable lesbian contingent in Chicago's Andersonville neighborhood (similar to Park Slope in Brooklyn). Despite this presence, there are no rainbow pylons along Clark Street, the Halsted-like main thoroughfare in Andersonville. Instead, Andersonville's lesbians, as well as those queer residents in other parts of the city, are expected to make a pilgrimage to Boystown in order to properly revel with pride.

To that end, there is a flagrant air of disdain and derision conveyed by many (white) queers who live in Boystown. These individuals view those of us who do not live in the gayborhood as lesser mortals. I reside on the opposite side of the city from Boystown and could not be happier. Boystown has, to me, a very insular feel. I cannot fathom why anyone who lives in one of the most diverse cities in the world would want to eat, sleep, work, party and do virtually everything else in the gay ghetto, rarely venturing out of its confines. Yet many queers who live in Boystown do just that. Their primary reason for doing so is that they feel "safer" in their own community. Whenever I hear this "safer" characterization, I quickly point out that for several years now, the majority of the hate crimes in Chicago leveled against queer people occur in Boystown—a statistic most neighborhood residents would like to forget.

Chicago is historically one of the more segregated cities in the US. Blacks live on the south side of the city, while whites have taken up residence on the city's north side. This culture of separatism reinforces white as the queer norm because white queers on the north side do not have to venture to the south side for queer culture. The city's designated queer area is literally in their front and back yards. Likewise, most blacks on the south side can point to Lakeview/Boystown and say, "The queer part of town?! That's on the north side where the white people live!" Thus, "queer," for many Chicagoans, is conflatedflated/equated with "white."

* * *

These sentiments do not just occur in isolation on the local level of Chicago. They reflect the ideology of a wide spectrum of the U.S.'s queer community. For example, where are the people of color on the cover of the *Advocate*, a publication that bills itself as "America's award-winning [queer] newsmagazine?" Even on the inside of the periodical—from the articles to the advertisements—there is limited representation of people of color. Why would any self-respecting (queer) person purchase, subscribe to, or revere a publication that does not represent them? Perhaps it would be wise for the editors of the *Advocate* to change their tagline to "White America's award-winning [queer] newsmagazine." It would certainly be more accurate.

The landscape of television is not much different in terms of representing queer people of color. The first such individual featured on *Queer As Folk* (the US version) was an Asian-American hustler. While I am sure there might be many hustlers of Asian descent, I would question having this caricature be a first in terms of representing racial and ethnic diversity within the queer community. Indeed, for some time now, I have thought television's main purpose is to distort reality. If that is true, it does its job exceedingly well. I have visited the cities of Pittsburgh and Toronto twice this year (where *Queer As Folk* is set and shot respectively) and I have yet to see anything in those cities resembling their *Queer As Folk* counterparts. If this is what constitutes entertainment, I am neither impressed nor amused.

Discussing the presence of queer characters on television, CNN recently observed:

> Prime-time television is getting "straighter" this year, with far fewer [queer] characters showing up on the fall schedule than appeared last season. . . . The number of [queer] characters in lead, supporting or recurring roles on network TV has dropped from twenty last year to just seven this coming season, according to an analysis by the Gay & Lesbian Alliance Against Defamation. . . . The decline, coming after three straight years in which [queer] characters enjoyed a surge in visibility on network television, was disappointing to leaders of the [queer] community. [According to Scott Seomin, media director for GLAAD,] "the diversity of the [queer] community cannot be conveyed through seven characters, *especially when all of those characters are white.*" (CNN.com; my emphasis)

Since television has a virtual stranglehold on contemporary popular culture, with most American households tuning in for a large portion of each day, it is imperative that viewers are aware of how the medium distorts. Taking into account the lack of LGBT characters as GLAAD has done as well as the concomitant scarcity of LGBT characters of color is one step towards this awareness.

It is refreshing to hear GLAAD take a stand with regard to unrealistic depictions of communities of color in the media and popular culture. I can recall an episode not so long ago when this same organization was unforgivably silent on the subject. In August 1998, the major motion picture *How Stella Got Her Groove Back* was released. The plot involves a single mother, the Stella of the title, who meets a much younger man while on vacation in the Caribbean. Upon her return to the States, Stella's sisters tease her about her May-December tryst. One of her siblings cautions Stella, apprising her that Jamaica is a haven for AIDS. Another sister sharply "corrects" her, informing her that it is in actuality the island of Haiti that is the disease's danger zone.

When I became aware of this stereotyped portrayal, I decided to contact GLAAD. Although the situation was not queer-specific, I thought—in keeping with their aim to fight defamation—the organization would have a vested interest in hearing about it. Consequently, I logged onto GLAAD's website and detailed the "Stella" mischaracterization in one of their action reports. After a few weeks had passed without response, I submitted an additional action alert also to no avail. At this point, nearly six weeks after the initial missive was sent and the movie had virtually disappeared from theatres, I dashed off a certified letter to GLAAD's Executive Director. At the time of this writing some four years later, I am still awaiting a reply.

Why was I irritated by this circumstance, you will ask. As an HIV-positive person, I think it is imperative for the media to represent AIDS accurately. The history of AIDS is the history of a disease rife with speculation and misinformation. I strongly believe that if the fictional Stella had vacationed in a notoriously queer hotspot, e.g., Palm Springs or Fire Island, and one of her sisters had made a statement associating one of those locales with white queers and AIDS, GLAAD's ire would have been raised. The fact that the organization was silent on the "Stella" issue—even though the organization is devoted to countering misrepresentation in the media—is telling.

This is certainly not the only lackluster response I have noted from a national queer organization. Consider the National Gay and Lesbian Task Force's (NGLTF) Annual Creating Chaos conference. (The name of the conference is really Creating Change, but I view it as Creating Chaos.) For several years now, the conference has included a People of Color Institute as part of its pre-conference proceedings. This institute commences and concludes before the conference's official kick-off. The underlying premise of this action reads, "Now that we've dispensed with the obligatory crap, we can proceed with the real issues at hand." I would like to know how NGLTF (or GLAAD or any other queer organization for that matter) can thoroughly discuss queer issues, can measurably create change, without fully integrating the concerns of queer people of color. It seems an impossibility to me.

In fairness, the theme of this year's Creating Chaos was "Building an Anti-Racist Movement: Working for Social and Economic Justice." But even with the adoption of this theme, the organization screwed things up months before the conference convened. At a meeting attended solely by leaders of queer statewide advocacy organizations, the Creating Chaos organizers encouraged each of those present to bring a person of color to the conference. If this was done, the organizers would waive the person of color's registration fees. This sounds perfectly fine until one realizes that some of the leaders of the statewide advocacy organizations are themselves people of color! Thus, should leaders like Latino Rick and black Gladys bring white people to Creating Chaos? Based on these examples, it should be readily apparent that some white queers have a—*excusez le mot*—fucked up idea of the diverse composition of the queer community. That these individuals are leaders in national queer organizations is all the more depressing.

Speaking of fucked up ideas of the queer community, I can think of no better candidate for the prize than the following. Early one morning in April 2001, I woke up and prepared to venture across town to the offices of the local queer advocacy organization. This was the organization's annual Lobby Day, wherein a group of a few hundred individuals travel to the state capital in support of a queer civil rights bill. The four-hour journey was made by a caravan of buses. I knew only one other person on my bus; accordingly, she and I talked with each other for the majority of the trip. As the buses neared our destination, we passed a road sign advertising Cracker Barrel restaurant, the chain notorious for discriminating against queers. At this moment, I was still engaged in conversation with my friend, although we had been joined by a newly-made acquaintance several moments before. Seeing the Cracker Barrel billboard, this latter individual stated, "I know you might not like this, but I hafta tell you a joke. What do you call a Cracker Barrel in a black community?" My friend and I exchanged glances. Before we had an opportunity to interrupt the jokester, he gleefully shared the "punch line": "A barrel of monkeys!"

This story is rife with implications in terms of what it reveals about the current state of racial and ethnic diversity within the queer community. How is it that anyone can make such a hurtful, racist utterance in the presence of others, particularly two individuals he had just met? How is it that he, a white person, could feel comfortable sharing this with me, a black person? Perhaps most importantly, how is it that this statement could be made under the auspices of going to advocate for a *civil rights bill*?

I believe this example underscores the crux of my argument quite handily in terms of what it reveals about the short-sightedness of white queers. These individuals can be so limited in their perspective that they disregard and alienate others with their insensitivity. This is not to say that *all* white queers have a propensity to be racially-obtuse, nor is my intent to devalue the opinions of white queers. Instead, I am emphasizing the collective onslaught of white queers' (racial) insensitivity. Whether it's an isolated incident like the "Barrel of Monkeys" debacle or the dearth of LGBT people of color in media outlets, the fact is that LGBT people of color oftentimes do not feel that we are valued members of the queer community, and more often than not, the reason for this sense of dissociation is the mindset and actions of white queers.

* * *

It bothers me when I hear white queers make statements like, "Being queer is exactly like being black, so mainstream society should give us laws and stop discriminating." It is not the same. In addition to the fact that this argument overlooks those of us who are black *and* queer, the bottom line is that I have an additional burden to bear. White queers rarely if ever have to think about how they are marginalized by virtue of their race. And they certainly don't make it easy for non-white queers to forget how our race is viewed as a liability. This is unfortunate because my race, which is oftentimes frowned upon in the queer community, is an inviolate and salient part of my identity. Just as I am disinclined to conceal my sexual orientation, I am surely not going to hide my race (presuming that I could). Therefore, I have no choice but to disagree when I hear white queers align their struggle with that of black individuals. Our stories are not identical for the simple reason that their blues ain't like mine.

We Don't Need No Hateration in this Dancery

By now, you are probably asking: what is the relevance of this to us here in Poland and/or Eastern Europe? I would respond by pointing out that since this book is predicated on the concept of putting an end to discrimination and marginalization, might I advocate we cease the same within the queer community? In so many instances, I am an invisible man in the queer community in which I live. The image of queer individuals that has been put forth for too long is one comprised of white people. This is erroneous and disrespectful. With this in mind, there may not be a large contingent of black people in your respective locales, but I encourage you to ask yourself: How many times have you treated someone discourteously because they are "different" from you based on a social construct? In your efforts to advocate for a community free of discrimination and marginalization, what kind of space are you truly creating? Who is allowed into this space? Who is excluded? Why?

As we work to create a world free of homophobia, we should remain cognizant of other oppressions, including those, particularly those, not experienced by us directly. This is a sentiment Suzanne Pharr conveys in her text *Homophobia: A Weapon of Sexism*, wherein she asserts:

> It is virtually impossible to view one oppression, such as sexism or homophobia, in isolation because they are all connected: sexism, racism, homophobia, classism, ableism, anti-Semitism, ageism. They are all linked by a common origin—economic power and control—and by common methods of limiting, controlling and destroying lives. There is no hierarchy of oppressions. Each is terrible and destructive. To eliminate one oppression successfully, a movement has to include work to eliminate them all or else success will always be limited and incomplete. (53)

Conclusion

This essay has only skimmed the surface of the rampant discrimination within the queer community. There are, to be sure, other facets of discrimination in addition to those I have discussed, e.g., age, socioeconomic status and class. It is important to remember that the queer community is multi-cultural, multi-layered, and multi-textured. This diversity is our biggest strength and asset. At the very least, we can respect, value and learn from one another.

I would like to conclude with an anecdote that encapsulates much of what I have said throughout this paper, and also offers a glimpse into the type of dangers I have identified if we cannot learn to respect one another. A few months ago, I was chatting with a friend who mentioned he had recently attended a meeting of queer bar owners in Boystown. My friend, who works for an AIDS service organization, asked the bar owners why they were not donating as much money to AIDS charities as they had in the past. The reason given—quite nonchalantly I might add—is that most of the money allocated to fight AIDS these days goes to black communities. The bar owners absolutely refused to devote their money to fighting AIDS in black communities.

    I suppose it did not occur to these bar owners that there might be black queer people or that queer white men are having sex with members of the black community or any of the other numerous, infinitesimal links between the two communities. Instead, their actions (or lack thereof) ignores the tide of the most deadly disease known to humankind all in an effort to preserve "their own." When you hear this story, I hope you realize it is a prime example of how communities can deteriorate internally. In essence, we may not have to look outside of the queer community for threats and intimidation, discrimination and marginalization. It might very well be that we are our own worst enemies.

Works Cited

Angelou, Maya. *The Heart of A Woman*. New York: Random House, 1981.
Ellison, Ralph. *Invisible Man*. New York: Random House, 1952.
"GLAAD: Gay presence on network TV down." 9.17.2002 <http://www.cnn.com/2002/-SHOWBIZ/TV/09/17/television.gays.reut/index.html>.
Hurston, Zora Neale. "How It Feels To Be Colored Me." *I Love Myself When I Am Laughing... And Then Again When I Am Looking Mean and Impressive: A Zora Neale Hurston Reader*. Ed. Alice Walker. New York: The Feminist Press at the City University of New York, 1979. 152-155.
Pharr, Suzanne. *Homophobia: A Weapon of Sexism*. Inverness: Chardon Press, 1988.

VIOLENCE AGAINST HOMOSEXUAL WOMEN: STORIES FROM EVERYDAY LIFE

IRINA KUPRIYANOVA

Nowadays the issue of violence against women is one of urgency. Discussed widely across the world, it has also become a serious concern in Russia. Violence against women is a gender-specific sort of aggression involving force and power exercised mostly by men against women. It includes verbal insults, threats, physical aggression, and sexual harassment. However, in Russia the problem has been discussed only in the context of heterosexual relations; I have not come across debates on the abuse of homosexual women. Meanwhile, homosexual women are among the victims and face greater risk than heterosexual women as their problems are invisible at first glance.

The elimination of all forms of violence should be analyzed from various perspectives. Since homosexual ways of living are not accepted by the heterosexual majority, sexual minorities are particularly vulnerable to acts of violence. Homosexual women experience double discrimination when sexism is compounded by homophobia. Moreover, many professionals who are obliged to deal with women in crisis fail to respond to the needs of homosexual women. There is a lack of knowledge about the lesbian self-image and life style among such practitioners as social workers, doctors, and psychologists. As Fran Walsh aptly observed, the "majority of current training programs in psychotherapy and consulting pay little (or even no) attention to issues of working with clients who are in violent relationships. Lack of knowledge in this sphere adversely affects the work of professionals and this is especially visible when it comes to clients with non-traditional sexual orientations" (Walsh 311-312). Consultants who lack such knowledge might be incompetent, prejudiced, and judgmental. To work professionally, a consultant should moreover clarify his/her own position towards homosexuality and be aware of stereotypes. What is the relation between violence and homosexuality?

Working at the Center for Social Problems and Humanitarian Development WINGS in Saratov, Russia I deal with homosexual women. The program "GOOD AS YOU" aims to help homosexual women exposed to all forms of public violence: psychological, emotional, physical, sexual, and economic. My experience confirms that problems of violence towards lesbians are very widespread and painful. The Center advises 10-15 homosexual women per month. One third of the reported problems concern violent incidents. Overall, the cases fall into the following categories: women abused by their sexual partners, domestic violence by other members of the family, acts of aggression perpetrated by the community or by homophobic groups, such as skinheads or criminals, and, finally, random violence.

Let me try to convey some of the stories from the everyday life of homosexual women who face these kinds of violence. In this study I used the narrative interview method to give women the opportunity to tell their stories, on the assumption that the narrative interview is a tool "that opens up new prospects for research on atypical experiences" (Iarskaia-Smirnova 122). The most frequent problem which women report are violent acts perpetrated by family members or friends—members of referent social groups. The reported incidents may have happened recently or a long time before the woman called the Center.

> CASE 1: And this so-called "girlfriend" stole my diary and brought it into our class. All the classmates read the diary and discussed it. When I came into the classroom, I saw the girls who were reading my diary and laughing. They noticed me and someone said, "Here she is." Then the hubbub began. I heard them say, "she is crazy," "she is mad," "she is a fool," and the most terrible words: "she is a lesbian!"
>
> I tried to get to my desk but they wouldn't let me pass. Everyone laughed. I began to feel faint; I didn't hear anything, only muttering. Then I was pushed by someone, and then pushed again and again, called foul things, insulted. I wanted to get out but they kept pushing me around and kept me inside. Then the worst thing happened. Someone struck me in the face. I tried to protect myself but it just made them angry. Everyone started to beat me and shout at me. Finally I fell down, but they did not stop. Then I couldn't resist any more. I wanted this to end, I kept thinking this was a dream and I would wake up. Then the bell rang. Everyone settled in their places while I remained down on the floor. Nobody helped me.
>
> The teacher came in and asked what had happened but they all said they didn't know. I wanted to speak out but couldn't so I just cried. The teacher helped me to tidy myself up and let me go home. Thank goodness my mother wasn't back from work and couldn't see me. I felt so bad, giddy. I was thinking about what to do now, how to live and why all these people are so malicious, why they had beaten me when I had not done anything bad. I wanted to take vinegar, I did not want to live, but then I remembered my mum and felt pity. When she came home I told her that I would not go to school any more.

This is a story of a girl who was abused by her classmates at a school to which she had recently moved. The only reason for the violence were her love letters addressed to a woman. The case illustrates the vulnerability of an adolescent with non-normative thoughts and feelings at a modern Russian school. Subsequently, the girl returned to the school but the school administration did not show any interest in the reported violence. It is quite common that parents and other relatives abuse women because of their actual or alleged homosexual identity. Such was the case of man who suspected his wife of "unauthorized" relations with her girlfriend. He isolated the woman from the outside world, denying her all forms of communication. Yet our client did not describe her husband's actions as violence: "There was no violence involved: he did not strike me at all." It is necessary to note that respondents have difficulty trying to define the situation of abuse. It very frequently happens that an incident is not recognized as violence, since violence is commonly understood as aggressive physical abuse.

The next story of a 28-year-old woman confirms that parents often react in an inappropriate way when their child's homosexuality is accidentally revealed.

> CASE 2: When my mother looked into the sauna, she saw a picture which did not leave any doubt as to what my girlfriend and I were doing. We were very excited and didn't even notice my mother. And it was so funny. . . . Back home in the evening my mother asked whether I'm a lesbian or not. I said that I am. She said that she and my father had suspected that for a long time but were afraid to ask. I asked her not to tell my father or anybody else about it. She promised she wouldn't. It seemed as if things had calmed down and were going fine. But everything good comes to an end. I don't know how it happened that my father found out we were intimate with N.
>
> He beat me violently, after saying that he would "beat the folly out of me," and that as long as I continued to "sit on his neck" I would have to be a normal woman who dates normal men, since it was high time for me to get married. Otherwise I could "go on to that. . . N." And if I didn't do as he said, I would no longer be a daughter to them, and so on. I could not go outdoors for a month afterwards because of the bruises, the shame, and the horror that everyone would point at me. I tried to be "normal". . .

The above case exemplifies almost all forms of violence: physical, psychological, and economic. Presumably violence was perpetrated because the aggressor (the father of the girl) demanded conformity to the stereotyped criteria of normality in order to preserve the family's status of "respectability." The situation is complicated by the fact that it was father who was the abuser, so the girl experienced the feelings of dependence, loneliness, and helplessness. As a result, she was in the position of a victim, trying to fulfill the requirements of the aggressor, to respond to his criteria of "normality," and to conceal the incident. Such situations are very common.

Other kinds of violence might be grouped under the category of "abuses in the mutual relations of partners." Violent incidents in homosexual relationships have much in common with those in heterosexual ones, yet there are differences. Let us turn to the experience of another respondent.

> CASE 3; We rented a flat and began to live together—what a dream! In the beginning everything was great, I was very pleased and happy that everything was cool. I did not notice the moment when our relations began to change; they must have changed gradually. I did not see that N. kept getting drunk more often. When she was heavily drunk, I overlooked her behavior and did not want to admit that everything was going to hell. When she was drunk, N. behaved differently; she became aggressive, malicious, she would get into a row at the slightest provocation. In the mornings, she would be kind, acting guilty, asking for forgiveness, and I did forgive her. . . . Then one fine day I found myself in hospital after being stabbed with a knife, and she was put in prison. Many times I wondered whose fault it was that things had turned out like that. I accused myself, her, the whole world, and then I realized that probably no-one was guilty. We had chosen this kind of relationship and this lifestyle because of our nature. Therefore there was nothing and nobody to complain about. It was probably our destiny. . .

In this case, the behavior of the victim and the abuser seems to be similar to the patterns of violence in heterosexual partnerships. Walsh confirms this observation, stating that homosexual women "feel very dependent and lonely after an incident not just because of the situation itself but because they do not have external support. Aggressors quite often deny their fault, accuse the victim, or blame what happened on the circumstances. Sometimes they openly deny the violence" (Walsh 318). However, violence in homosexual relationships is essentially different in that it results from homophobia, both external and internalized. Homophobia is often internalized unconsciously, but since it resides in all homosexual people to a greater or lesser extent, it needs to be taken into account in work with homosexuals.

Today's social life in Russia is such that violence against homosexual people is actually encouraged; in some subcultures this is reflected in a hypertrophied way.

> CASE 4: You know, they believe it is a sign of special prowess, almost a feat, to rape a lesbian. And those "frostbites" [Russian jargon for people who have no moral values, whose soul is frozen] came to our summer house and in the beginning everything was all right. We talked, remembered our childhood. He spoke about his life "in the zone" [in prison]. We were drinking of course. Then N. proposed sex. I refused. Then we drank once more and he glanced at me, saying something like: "Hey, guys, I know she is a lesbian. Don't you want to try sex with a lesbian?" The men started to laugh out loud and demand the proof of my heterosexuality. I tried to turn this into a joke but N. said: "If you do not want

to do it the friendly way, we'll have to do it the rough way," and he raped me in full view of the others. Then he suggested that his friends should "try out the lesbian" and they were easily persuaded. All this proceeded till morning. Maybe it's my fault that I didn't scream; I just prayed that L. [the respondent's girlfriend] would not happen to come by and get caught up in this nightmare. I did not scream because N. said to me, "Keep quiet, otherwise it will get worse." Before leaving, they threatened that if I told anybody, things would get worse—they might even kill—me, so I have not told anybody about it.

At the Center we have also come across manifestations of violence "by mistake," when homosexual women were taken for homosexual men.

CASE 5: We shaved our heads and put on bandanas. At first glance we looked like boys, though our faces looked feminine, and we were perceived by the public, especially by youths, as a couple of gay guys. This had odd consequences. Here we were. And for some reason the groups of guys we ran into reacted very negatively. They called us things like "damned perverts," "pederasts," and so on, and said, "Come here. We will bla-bla-bla you right and left." Here we were. And these were people hardly older than ourselves, probably around 30, adult guys whose lives we had somehow disrupted.

It's interesting that one day I was traveling by train and a group of teenagers also took me for a gay guy. They pointed their fingers at me, discussed something in an agitated way. It was very strange. I had not expected that people who do not behave in an obnoxious way, who just look a little like somebody, can disturb others. Then, when I got up, they all saw the parts of my body that suggest I'm female. Everyone somehow calmed down and the tension was diffused; they merely turned away, that's all. . .

When we attempted to analyze the everyday-life stories of homosexual women focusing on violence, it became clear that there is a need for the qualified help of social workers, psychologists, lawyers, and physicians. In our earlier research we had discovered professionals' discriminatory attitudes towards clients during the process of interpersonal consultation. We also found that professionals are often unaware of their own discriminatory attitudes. Moreover, consulting is not free from gender stereotypes associated with patriarchal culture. Such stereotypes affect clients and adviser-client relations. There is a discrepancy between the advisers' verbal statements about non-discriminatory work and the practice of consulting.

Consequently, we think professionals should adopt the following principles for non-discriminatory work in dealing with homosexual women who have been exposed to violence:

- reject patriarchal attitudes;

- aim to establish equal mutual relations with the client and give priority to the client's system of values;
- respect the client's life-style;
- not work with a client if the counsel's system of values is in opposition to the client's;
- be aware of one's own attitudes towards such basic issues as: life style, social and marital status, gender characteristics, cultural features;
- be aware that the non-traditional or non-normative styles of interpersonal relations may give rise to an alternative set of social values and cultural paradigms, as well as an alternative way of living;
- be open to alternative styles of interpersonal relations and avoid imposing traditional social attitudes on all people.

Dominic Davis points out that "working with people whom the professional cannot consider with sufficient respect, and whose system of values contradicts his/her own, is a manifestation of professional incompetence" (Davis 67). Professionals who work with abused women have to be prepared to listen to non-prevailing opinions, and to recognize the value of other ways of thinking, in order to understand the meaning and value of the experience and relationships of people with non-normative sexual orientations.

Our conclusions about the practice of abuse of homosexual women are as follows:

- violence against homosexual women is an urgent social problem which requires reflection and action;
- violent practices occur in all spheres of life: violence may take place within the parental family, the immediate community, and in lesbian partnerships; there is institutionalized homophobia, violence by aggressive and homological groups or individuals, as well as «random» violence;
- sometimes incidents are not recognized as violence; speaking about their experiences of abuse, some clients did not understand that violence had taken place, treating such situations as typical, inevitable, or normal;
- to work successfully with homosexual women it is necessary to take into account their social experience, gender characteristics, institutional and internalized homophobia, social and cultural context;
- following non-discriminatory principles is fundamental in working with homosexual women clients.

Works Cited

Davis, Dominic. "Sozdanie modeli affirmativnoi gay-psihoterapii" [Model of affirmative gay—psychotherapy]. *«Rozovaya psihoterapiya»: Rukovodstvo po rabote s seksual'nymi men'shinstvami* ["Pink psychotherapy": the Management on work with sexual minority]. Ed. D.Davis, Ch.Nil. Saint Petersburg: Piter, 2000.

Iarskaia-Smirnova, Elena. *Odezhda dlya Adama i Evy. Ocherki gendernyh issledovanii* [Clothes for Adam and Eve]. Moscow: RAN YuNION, Saratov: Gos. Tehn. Unt. Centr soc. politiki i gendernyh issled., 2001.

Walsh, Fran. "Zloupotrebleniya vo vzaimootnosheniyah partnerov" [Abuse in partnerships]. *«Rozovaya psihoterapiya»: Rukovodstvo po rabote s seksual'nymi men'shinstvami* ["Pink psychotherapy": the Management on work with sexual minority]. Ed. D.Davis, Ch.Nil. Saint Petersburg: Piter, 2000.

SEX SLAVERY AND QUEER RESISTANCE IN EASTERN EUROPE[1]

TOMEK KITLIŃSKI, JOE LOCKARD

Fourteen years into the transition from the communist system, eastern Europe is undergoing an economic and ideological crisis. Unemployment, poverty, and homelessness are mounting. The fragile and very limited democracy wants to pass for macho. It is categorically straight, and in general, hostile to minorities.

The Holocaust and communism put an end to multiculturalism, and after 1989 the 'resurrected' states invested in their mythic identity and monolithic 'national spirit.' The Baltics, when independent, desired to build mono-ethnic nation-states, which resulted in Russians being stripped of citizenship in Estonia. A number of post-communist countries overflow with hatred towards their Roma population. Liberalization processes initiated by legal reforms attendant to EU membership have not changed these underlying social animosities. Indeed, the EU's envoy to Slovakia, Eric Van der Linden, neatly demonstrated that political Europeanization can provide one more platform for the same manifest racism when he called for the removal of Roma children from their parents and forcible placement in boarding schools to learn "European values" (*New York Times*, May 14, 2004).

The new republics are far from welcoming strangers: they fear their purity may be soiled by the inclusion of others and excel in entrenching themselves against foreign invasions. As it invents new social defenses against contagion, eastern Europe is engaged simultaneously in a master-slave dialectic with the US and the EU: civic sadomasochism, one that inflicts and welcomes social pain, characterizes its bodies politic. Eastern Europe today is filled with growing legions of unemployed and poor, the disposable people, the neo-slaves—Turgenevev's *lishnye ludi* of the nineteenth century. The economics and poetics of sadomasochism persist now as they did then; the serfdom of eastern Europe continues and its international slavery deepens.

New capitalism in eastern Europe is a new form of slavery: political and military slavery to the US, economic slavery to corporations, and cultural slavery to coca-colonization. This old-new Second World remains a dumping ground of goods and a cheap-labor workshop for the West, one with the added advantage of breeding reliable cannon fodder for imperialist wars. And don't we enjoy slavery? Montaigne's partner, Etienne de La Boetie, wrote about *volonté de servir*. The master seduces us, writes La Boetie in the sixteenth century, but aren't we seduced too? The very name "masochism" comes from eastern Europe, the borderlands of Ukraine and Poland where Leopold von Sacher-Masoch was born and bred and returned to this area in his erotic fictions, among them *Venus in Furs*. Sacher-Masoch wrote about sex slavery in the seductive thrall of *femmes fatales* who are in turn slaves of the male imagination. Today the seductions of free-market capitalism involve *volonté de servir* and eastern bodies/labor organized to offer servitude to western capital. The pleasures are neither equal nor voluntary; we live amid scenarios of civic sadomasochism.

The Poetics of Civic Sadomasochism

Eastern Europe's subordination is a feminized or festishized position: domestic slavery in the world order. East Europeans are trained in capitalism and militarism while they are slowly initiated into the 'free world' of the EU and NATO. This is their coming of age. The rites of passage for eastern Europe require a great deal of preparation, meeting of criteria, schooling, and proper cultural dress. Under the paternal instruction of Westerners, Easterners are expected to mature in their Foucauldian 'docile bodies.' (No wonder that Foucault started his career on a diplomatic mission in Poland.) Eastern Europe is perceived as recipient of aid, discipline, and limited empowerment. It is not an agent, but a submissive partner in global sex.

If eastern Europeans are exploited, at the same time, they (we) dehumanize others. Desire coupled with repulsion dehumanizes and demonizes its object. The slaves of our desire-revulsion are turned into refuse. The desired bonding with the West is a same-sex fantasy, a repressed homosexuality within, which results in homophobia without. It is a combinatory hallucination of Hollywood and the Catholic Church—a gay homogeny that denies itself and denies the rights of others. Male bonding with the West consists in sadomasochistic bondage, a fantasy that war realizes. Intervening in Iraq, the US bonded with Poland, culminated same-sex military desires, and realized male dreams of torturing and killing and fucking—each other and together. Poland is the bottom here, the slave; but the slaves of America, Poland's masters, are tops at home. The violent dominances of the Al Ghraib prison's forced and staged homosexual scenes were being played out through international and domestic symbolism long before these dull military jailors employed them literally.

Eastern Europe is riveted by war, sadomasochism, and psychomachia. Poland is brutalized and brutalizes itself. Poland spreads its buttocks for the US and at the same time rapes its own minorities; Poland is colonized and colonizes;

Poland is penetrated and penetrates unwilling partners. This is (self-) enslavement; it is reification of humanity coupled with xenophobic dumping to create 'human refuse,' and it is the same processes that create a domestic regime of legal tolerance for sexual enslavement. The proletarianization of Poland, slavery of women and sexual minorities, violent hate of numberless 'others,' and theocracy are coupled with militarism, involvement in the Iraq invasion, economic globalization, coca-colonization. The transition has been from communism to fundamentalism-cum-McWorld.

Hegel's dialectic of master and slave is particularly relevant. Ukrainian-born Alexandre Kojève's reading of Hegel accentuated what we read here as civic sadomasochism. Freud, from out of a *mittel*-Europe ripped ceaselessly by masculinist militarism, defined armies as libidinous union. With such a libidinal anchor, the army reiterates the primal horde, its violence, and male sexual competition. Kristeva argues that society has changed into the dialectic of master and slave. In our view, sadomasochism rules that dialectic. The sexuality of militaries and paramilitaries prevails in eastern Europe.

One manifestation of this phenomenon is *fala*, the 'wave,' an unofficial system of dependency upon surveillance, control, abuse, and torture of—as if Gramsci had predicted it—the subaltern. The slavery of Eastern Europe, the *fala*, is degradation. It is a mafia-esque S&M pecking order that originated in militaries, entered schools, and now is a social system of the Second World. *Fala* reflects eastern Europe's feudalism (serfdom ended in 1861 in Russia and in 1864 for Russian Poland) and the traditional sex roles of eastern Europe, restored by the transition.

Fala is sadomasochistic and systemic; it dwells on sexual intimidation, individual and mass. It employs bullying, torture, and ritual S&M for sexual subjugation; it is a duel between competing desires. Voluntary or involuntary, penile or penal servitude—the slavery of eastern Europe is sexual humiliation. Both the sadist and the masochist feel in charge, in control. Theodor Reik writes about the hubris of the masochist, but maybe sadism and masochism are reversible and forever combined. "Ein Sadist ist immer ein Masochist. Ein Masochist ist immer ein Sadist," according to Freud's diagnosis.

Eastern Europe co-opts the sadomasochism—sadism and masochism in one—of militarized global culture; eastern Europe both receives and inflicts globalist pain. Poland delights in suffering: partitions, hopeless uprisings, failed fights. *Gloria victis* was the old national slogan: glory to those who failed. It has been renewed by the all-male eastern European political triumvirate of party, militia, and mafia who use *fala*, either implicitly or explicitly, to evoke fear and exert control. Their passionate sadomasochistic affair with the US has only reinvigorated the *fala* with US-manufactured social Viagra for extra energy.

Maltreatment of the subaltern in the army, prisons, and schools produces a sadomasochistic language. Not only Russia, but also Poland has adopted the intensely lewd, ithyphallic, S&M language of the prisons. Its use is, as Victor Erofeyev writes, a linguistic show of power; the language reflects the full spectrum of ethnic and gender hatreds. Not only is *kurwa* (lowest bitch, cheapest hooker) a common conversational filler (the current hit of Poland's cinema dialogs is "what do you, *kurwa*, know about killing?"), but a number of verbs like *jebac* incorporate 'fucking, beating, thrashing' inside one term. Prejudice is cultivated through a nonchalant etiquette of linguistic brutalization; language itself has become *fala*.

Pervasive abusive language is indicative of gender-class abjection, of opinions on the proper uses for "bitches, faggots, and kikes." In Poland, lesbians and gays are denied human rights because their claims of humanity are refused. The social transition has gone wrong: it is majoritarian absolutism. Totalitarianism gave way to fundamentalism. Transition has meant liberalization (free elections, travel) without sexual freedom. Mainstream media, in particular the state media, foreground mainstream sexuality. There is no *Queer Eye for the Straight Pole* here. Poland's body politic is heterosexual, or rather, heterosocial. Sexophobia under communism has heightened in post-communism. There is a rising resentment against women and homosexuals, and the immobility of Polish politics blocks inclusion of sexual minorities.

Aging Dissidents in Status Quo Drag

In eastern Europe the once-dissident class, whether the elegant Havel or the stumbling Walesa, now do not dissent but conform; they have been seduced by the West. They are ready to seduce their own societies, in whose maturity they do not believe, in order to submit them to Western repression. But they also remain slaves to their own traditions of feudalism and strict class hierarchies of the inter-war and even the communist period. Populists and ex-dissidents argue that eastern Europe is a special case due to successive and prolonged political repressions. Yet as Renata Salecl notes, eastern Europeans insist on preservation of cultural difference when it is an advantage in preserving their traditional patriarchal structures.

Polish dissidents delight in their own men's house culture. They were never pacifist or feminist. Their aim was to re-decorate *status quo ante* communism, to reproduce the male-dominated past beneath a post-modern pastiche. Machismo could be restored and it was in 1989: man-to-man, but heterosexist law and order. Men fuck-kill men in secret, but reject the rights of gays; these same men reject the rights of women too.

Dissidents share with skinheads of the resurgent militias a phobia of women and gays; a homosocial principle runs deep between them. From scouting to patriarchal education to sport, dissidents move within a cult of maleness. Domination, submission, and re-achievement of domination marks their historiographic trajectory. They submit to the West and the Church while they dream of dominating women; they dominate bodies to the point of denying women's control of their own bodies (abortion). In their boasts, dissidents are lady-killers; in their writings, they are squeamish, priggish, and prudish. Their puritanism complements the patriarchal teachings of the Church. The club of dissidents follows the homosociality of the Church and the army; it is a herd of sameness. Here one can wrestle to become master and/or slave; here one can gratify hostility and a hankering for fellow-men. There is no place for women and gays who lead the nation—and Western culture—astray.

Dissidents aimed to break single-party communist domination but enslaved themselves to the ideology and practice of 'free market democracy,' that is, economic imperialism. Their anti-communist militancy changed into pro-US militancy, by no means a necessary political logic. Rather, the official dissident class has always been nostalgic for elitist nostrums of the Western tradition, for a humanistic canon that protected their class status. Before 1989, dissidents limited their politics to fighting the system and found an alternative in the repressions of the opposing camp; women or minorities with their rights need not apply. They believed in the power of high culture, Church, and perennial truths. Analyses of class, the unconscious, gender and sexuality were beyond their pale.

Eastern European herself, Julia Kristeva had no illusions about anti-communist dissidents when she wrote in 1977 that the political dissident "still remains within the limits of the old master-slave couple" (Kristeva 295). Some dissidents "retain a certain nostalgia for community and law, and find a substitute in orthodox religion" (Kristeva 299). In their self-regard as the last keepers of the flame of Western culture, this ex-dissident class renders themselves slavish imitators and the perfect submissives in a sadomasochistic drama.

Poland in Imperial Leather

On May 1, 2004, as Poland joined the European Union, it was relishing its sadomasochistic affair with the United States. Even as Poland is in the midst of economic and political crises, marching out with American crusaders has raised national hopes. As Poland dresses in imperial leather and sends the army abroad, on the home front global moral salvation is the message of the day. "I give you a challenge, Poland. Please be a world leader in solving homosexuality," US 'conversion therapist' Richard Cohen told Poland on the fundamentalist Radio Maryja. Cohen's message was heard not only on radio, but also in the halls of the Polish parliament, as the far-right League of Polish Families invited Cohen to give a presentation there.

In this New Straight Order, true male friends know their subordinate duties; Patroclus stands to fight alongside his lover Achilles. President Bush demanded loyalty from the leading 'New Europe' ally after fey Spain's limp socialist-led withdrawal, and the Polish president let fade his remarks that Poland had been "misled" on Iraq. With its flag flying at Camp Babylon, Poland is truly under the hallucination of globalist conversion therapy. How is Poland, a country with twenty per cent unemployment and widespread poverty, to lead the world in military support of US policy? Bush and hetero-*macher* Cohen together mislead the world into believing that dominant hatreds are right.

Yet in spite of the pope's opposition to the intervention in Iraq, the Polish Church endorses it. Erotic pictures of Polish boys in the media accompany images of chaplains blessing the men before action. A Polish news channel broadcast Christmas midnight mass at Camp Babylon. A media trumpeter for Bush's war policy, the Polish status-equivalent of the *New York Times*, *Gazeta Wyborcza* returned to its prejudices of the 1990s. Propagandistically pro-American when Poland first occupied Iraq, *Gazeta Wyborcza* offered platitudes of pro-intervention propaganda. When Saddam was captured, *Gazeta* ran a caption under a front-page photograph of him being examined: "Saddam Hussein is checked for lice." *Gazeta* neglects the grave crises of Polish society: intractable unemployment, massive discrimination and violence against women, and the spread of working-class neo-slavery. Generally, with very little critical reporting, the media support the neo-slavery superstructure and base of Poland.

Poland's state TV glamorizes, eroticizes, and homoeroticizes the image of Polish troops in Iraq: young men in fatigues, young men without fatigues, young men shirtless, young men under the shower. A gang strip-tease of a Polish platoon. Cameraderie is cultivated soldier-to-soldier, but *esprit de corps* enlarges into international pacts and the homosociality of NATO into which eastern Europe is now being admitted. Mateship is mating; it produces the manpower needed for sex and war. This is the place to crack the whip—between Johnny and Janek, between Washington and Warsaw.

Every Sunday evening Poland's national TV broadcasts a documentary (or rather, a reality TV serial) entitled *babilon.pl*. The very title denominates Iraqi territory as a Polish colony, as Babylon colonized by the Internet country domain 'pl' for Poland. In its latest installment, *babilon.pl* featured Polish troops caring for Iraqi children, bringing them sweets, mascots, and exercise books. "Good mistah," says an Iraqi kid of a Polish soldier, much like the "Mistah Kurtz" of Polish writer, Joseph Conrad. The colonized are infantilized: children are children and they dominate the film. But the larger message is that not only are all Iraqis children, indeed all Arabs are children. Colonial militarism demands subordinate subjects for its pedophilic *mission civilatrice*, and Iraq provides a fresh supply.

These are systemic manifestations of the construction of a cultural market for domination and subordination, a symbolic slave market. This market held alongside the imperial parade-ground desires not only external but internalized sameness, especially gendered and sexual. Control of sexuality is a crucial ideological feature that determines who will be the masters of this market. Throughout eastern Europe parties of the right continue their crusade against contraception, abortion, and sex education. In Poland, Lithuania, Slovakia and Croatia, politicians render Catholicism into a sexophobic ideology. Women's rights are used as tools, if not toys, in the hands of extremists. Women are not true owners of their bodies—the body politic deprives women and gays of the right to equal bodies. Those beyond heteronormativity are perceived as aliens.

After the fall of Communism, this social transit towards majoritarian absolutism in Poland has been facilitated by the forcible and increasing grip of religion-turned-ideology. Adoption of the imperial manner has been aided by the appropriation of religion in support of theocratic political ambitions, a strategy underwritten by ex-dissidents in public office. In 1990, religious instruction was introduced into schools without parliamentary debate. In 1992, parliament passed the Respect for Christian Values in Mass Media Act. In 1993, abortion was banned. In 1993, the Polish government signed a concordate with the Vatican; the parliament ratified it in 1998. Polish politicians and ex-dissidents out-pope (and out-Pole) the Polish pope.

Empires of monolithic national-religious spirit, sexual totalitarianism, and free-market capitalism are being built simultaneously.

Sex Slave Proletariat

Eastern Europe has become the sexual playground of the West. Kosovo, Poland, the Czech Republic, and the Ukraine are exploited for sexual trafficking, prostitution, and the sex industry. The Czech Republic and western Poland are used for Western tourism, hetero- and homosexual alike. Traffic operates in all directions: an estimated quarter of the prostitutes in Germany are from eastern Europe, and one recent MSNBC report estimates that a tenth of Moldova's female population has been sold into prostitution as a national 'export product.'

The value hierarchy of sex diminishes eastwards, as bodies become ever-cheaper. Sex slavery couples with national-economic-linguistic servitude: predictably, wealthy Finland has its Estonian slaves. Gayatri Chakravorty Spivak notes that the ex-Soviet republic of Estonia is being colonized by Finland

(Spivak 28). At the same time as Polish "docile bodies" are enslaved by social injustices, Poles are becoming masters of Ukrainian prostitutes. Ukraine is abused by the Poles; Ukrainian prostitutes are in Polish brothels, on Polish streets and highways. In this enchained hierarchy, the terms of sexual proletarianization intensify with distance from rich western European centers of capital.

Western militarization furthers this objectification of women as gratification available for cheap purchase. *The Guardian* (May 7, 2004) reports "Western troops, policemen and civilians are largely to blame for the rapid growth of the sex slavery industry in Kosovo over the past five years, a mushrooming trade in which hundreds of women, many of them under-age girls, are tortured, raped, abused and then criminalized." In Bosnia in 2002, over 180 employees of Dyncorp, a US military contractor for helicopter maintenance, were implicated in a sex slavery ring.

Social reproduction of masculinist violence gains transmission through gender-class, and reproduces unending trauma in its women victims. Integration into the neo-liberal sphere has provided traffickers with a new mode of expanding an annual traffic, one whose dimensions are estimated variously between several hundred thousand to one million women. This is a repetition of an earlier trafficking history: in the late nineteenth and early twentieth centuries eastern European Jewish women were so prevalent throughout the Latin American sex industry that *polaca* was a common term for 'prostitute.' Religious and social contempt, dissolving family structures, and desperate poverty created this history, and then are recurring today. Intensification of economic repression focuses on gender-class targets vulnerable to coercion and violent exploitation. Tina Modotti called women "the proletariat of the proletariat." The tide of trafficked women's bodies to service the pyramid of global desire has created an international proletariat of women, and proletariats burn with their own special anger.

Religious Sadomasochism and Counter-Art

Toleration of such civil sadomasochism against the women of eastern Europe reflects the region's having been taken hostage by an unholy trinity of mafias, clerical parties, and former dissidents-turned-devout. The prevailing public ideology has close kinship with the sadomasochistic ideas of Mel Gibson; his blood-adoring version of Catholicism is used to confirm hatreds of 'otherness.' Gibson's *Passion* became the favorite of Poland's Catholic clergy and congregations. The faithful are bused into movie theaters to weep throughout *The Passion of the Christ*.

Cardinal Jozef Glemp, head of the Polish Church, found the film "pre-eminent"; the director of the Catholic ultra-right Radio Maryja, Father Tadeusz Rydzyk, deemed it "arch-beautiful." What one sees in the film though is not body beautiful, but a bloody pulp; it represents the fulfillment, according to psychoanalyst Klaus Theweleit, of xenophobic and totalitarian fantasies. And this sadistic scene provides eastern Europe's phantasmagoria of enslavement and its true path towards liberation.

From the seventeenth century on, Poles believed Poland to be the Messiah of the peoples. The seventeenth-century invention of Poland as the Messiah inaugurated xenophobia in Poland, the repression of 'others'—dissenters (*dysydenci* or *innowiercy*—'other-believers' in Polish), as they were called. Baroque messianism and hatred of the 'other-believers,' Romantic worship of Napoleon, and anti-communist opposition formed the cumulative historical background. In the context of this ever-present tradition, Gibson's *The Passion of the Christ* in Poland is no innocent business; its preaching reinforces the deeply conservative Catholic monopoly. This is a region of Europe where there is special strength to a calendar and its imagery, from Redeemers to Passions, a region that Emmanuel Levinas saw as saturated with a "Christian atmosphere" (qtd. in Pollock 159). As Jewish and feminist art historian Griselda Pollock asks, "What narratives of history can reclaim for memory the forgotten and the lost without subjecting Jewish grief to an alien, Christian or Greek imaginary?"

The "oblivion of Jews and women in culture" (Pollock 116) is particularly grave, in fact tragic, in Poland. But counter-stories and challenges to the causations of such oblivion find little or no public space. Recently a young artist, Dorota Nieznalska, was sued and sentenced for her installation *Passion* in Gdansk. League of Polish Families members attacked Nieznalska verbally and physically at the Gdansk gallery where her installation was being exhibited last year. The work, an exploration of masculinity and suffering, shows a cross on which a photograph of a fragment of a naked male body, including the genitalia, has been placed. The League sued the artist. In July 2003, a court found Nieznalska guilty of "offending religious feelings." It sentenced her to half a year of "restriction of freedom" (she was specifically banned from leaving the country) and ordered her to do community work and pay all trial expenses. When the judge read the sentence, League members packing the courtroom applauded ecstatically. The artist has been pursuing legal appeal to get the sentence overturned on free speech grounds.

Instead of Nieznalska's artwork, Gdansk, the city of the Solidarity movement, had Gibson-inspired Easter decoration this year. In St. Bridget's basilica, a former Solidarity shrine, the tradition of sepulchers where the figure of Jesus is entombed on Good Friday foregrounded the anti-Jewish motto that even Mel Gibson edited out of the English translation of *The Passion*: "His blood be on us, and on our children" (Matthew 27: 25). In the country of the unmourned losses of Jews, the prelate of St. Bridget's added a commentary on the sepulcher: "Jews killed Lord Jesus and the Prophets and they persecute us, too." With such inscriptions the Catholic faithful are re-imagined as the suffering subjects of a malignant and present force, part of a sadistic continuum from the Bible to the present. The imagination of persecution specifies an imaginative necessity for suffering, the central necessity of sadomasochism.

One young artist, Tomasz Kozak, satirizes such national myths; in fact, he psychoanalyzes them. Kozak, a painter, cartoonist and video artist, provides rare homoerotically-informed analyses of eastern European chauvinism and sexuality. One of the pieces banned in the Center for Contemporary Art in Warsaw (predictably, since it banned Andres Serrano's 'Piss Christ' years ago, and last year banned persons under age 21 from an exhibition of Nan Goldin's queer photography) was Kozak's painting, entitled 'Self-Portrait with the Only Property.' It depicts the only property left to young Poles: their anal sexuality to be penetrated and enslaved. It enters the anal sadomasochism of eastern Europe and plays against representations of hysteria in the iconography of la Salpêtrière's male patients, where they spread their legs awaiting intercourse and at the same time defend themselves against it. Kozak's critique of the militaristic values that dominate Poland caricatures the anal examinations conducted by medical draft boards that authorize obligatory conscription-enslavement. It is a position for and against fuck-beat-thrash *jebac*. Kozak's work attacks Poland's militarism and its entry into a global military order; he rejects a national embrace, in his words, of "wars and lechery: nothing else holds fashion."

Yet it is too simple to continue to enumerate sadistic and masochistic sources of social oppression, as against individual counter-voices. Outlining broader emergent blocs and forms of cultural resistance is a more ambiguous undertaking, since it traces out shadows—powerful shadows, nonetheless—against substance.

Queering the Polish Academy

Democracy does not mean unmitigated majority rule, but recognition and cultivation of minorities. Writing in *The Guardian*, Brian Whitaker argues "there are always governments seeking to make exceptions to the principle of universality." Under the umbrella of religious or cultural norms, discrimination is promulgated through the delimitation of cultural contingency. The Polish academy is a major center for advancing rationales for discrimination, though it can also be a center for its reversal.

In Poland, former dissidents come into social authority now indulge in disputes over the limits of toleration. Their majoritarian tone resonates time and again in Polish debates over education. For example, Andrzej Koźmiński, a recent conference panelist discussing the *Open the Social Sciences* reform report, held that although the idea of diversity is worth pursuing, it should be cleansed of *dziwactwa* ('eccentricities, quirks, queers' Flis 184). Another speaker, Andrzej Flis, called the contemporary position of universities "pathological" when, as he claimed, "a self-respecting faculty at a decent university must have an African-American, a few women, including a lesbian or a mute. A key for recruiting has been established that foregrounds characteristics which are absolutely inessential to the production of knowledge" (Flis 177-178).

Recently in an essay in the influential daily *Rzeczpospolita*, political philosopher Ryszard Legutko recently called scholars of queer studies 'parasites'—a recourse to Stalinist terminology, when political enemies were routinely accused of social parasitism. It was the same philosophy professor who authored a collection of essays nonchalantly entitled *I Don't Like Toleration*. The *Rzeczpospolita* essay referred to gays as "people of a disturbed sphere of sexual desire" and mocked LGBT studies: "There is a mania of looking for homosexual subtexts in many creators of culture. No small legion of university parasites tries to make careers based on such research" (Legutko).

Despite the historical pronouncements of its narrow-minded religio-ethnic nationalists, eastern Europe has not nearly the tradition of civic antagonism towards homosexuality that they posit. Both Samuel Collins and Adam Olearius, seventeenth-century English travelers in eastern Europe and Russia, commented on the relative open-ness and tolerance of homosexuality and expressed surprise that "Sodomy and Buggery" (Collins) were not capital offenses as in England. Neither does 'eastern Europe' represent a monolithic sexual culture inasmuch as Orthodox canon law, influenced by Hellenistic and early Christian gender concepts, has been significantly more tolerant than the Catholic Church (although it should be noted that last year, in a fit of official pique, the Russian Orthodox Church not only defrocked a priest in Nizhny Novgord who performed the marriage ceremony for two gay men but also demolished the 'desecrated' Chapel of the Vladimir Icon of the Mother of God where the ceremony was held). The Polish academy, historically aligned with and sponsored by the Church, has adopted the less-tolerant Catholic tradition.

The consequences of anti-gay public attacks by senior academics were soon felt. The day of publication, the chair of the Department for Polish Culture at Warsaw University denied lecture halls for the continuation of a series of extracurricular lectures in queer studies, entitled "Homosexuality in Culture" and organized at the initiative of department students. The first and, as it turns out, last lecture was held by Paweł Leszkowicz on the critical art of New York City gay artist and activist, David Wojnarowicz. The lectures were scheduled to include the subjects of literature, cinema, philosophy, ethics and cultural anthropology in LGBT studies and run throughout the semester. It is equally indicative that when Leszkowicz sent his writing on Wojnarowicz's retrospective in SoHo's New Museum to *Gazeta Wyborcza*, he received the following e-mail response from an editor: "Even if they are called the worst obscurantists in the world, our photo editors do not allow such art in our magazine."

Yet counter-posed to the attitude of gay-rejectionist venues, a first collection of LGBT essays in Polish, *A Queer Mixture*, was published and another is forthcoming. Annual international queer studies conferences and an increasing number of interdepartmental queer studies seminars, with funding from university rectors, constitute part of this new visibility. A new wave of queer art is emerging from university art departments and galleries.

The academy provides fora for oppositionalist public intellectuals in Poland, and women scholar-activists contribute some of the leading voices of dissent. Last year Maria Szyszkowska, a professor of law and philosophy and senator in parliament, introduced a legislative proposal for registered same-sex partnership bill, one based on Germany's Act of Life Partnership. While there is very little chance for the passage of such an act, the European Parliament may force the Polish government's hand. The 2002 report on Fundamental Rights in the EU endorsed same-sex marriage and adoption rights for homosexuals, and the EU's Court of Human Rights has ruled repeatedly in support of equal rights for gays. The commitment of a parliamentarian and academic such as Szyszkowska towards achieving equal rights represents what can be achieved through the use of academia to reform public policy. This confluence of public culture and grassroots activism inside universities has had and will continue to have profound social effects.

Queer Slave Revolt

In classical Marxist thought slavery is a mode of production that characterizes primitive communities, feudalism, and pre-industrial agrarian societies. It disappears with the advent of industrial modes of production, replaced by wage labor that constitutes a more efficient mode of social organization for extracting surplus value from labor. This analytic model is flawed because it posits a teleological annunciation of slavery's end. Marx, writing as a journalist observing the American civil war, analyses it flatly as a sectional conflict between Northern industrialism and Southern slave oligarchy. For this model, the inherent feudalism of slavery as a mode of production interferes with creation of a fluid labor force and condemns it to termination by capitalism, which operates through control of labor rather than absolute ownership of bodies. Remnant slaveries are marginal to history under industrialized modes of production. The constitutional abolition of slavery, Marx argued in an 1862 *Die Presse* article, was only a prelude to "the revolutionary waging of war." Slavery's abolition, in such analyses, constitutes a predictive historical dividing line in the progress of national social institutions rather than a moment in a continuing emancipatory contest involving a wide spectrum of slaveries.

In our view, slavery does not fade into history. Complete abolition is no more possible than perfected human liberation. Slavery lies in wait; it emerges in fits and starts; it re-invents itself in continual neo-slaveries; it is part of the human condition. Modes of production foster or diminish enslavements; they do not eliminate the phenomenon. Slavery emerges from powerful psychological forces in the unconscious, and consequently is part of the political unconscious that constantly re-emerges into public expression. Slavery employs, even arguably equals, masochism. It operates through individual and social desires to create obedient submission, and to create in others a will to submit.

Gender-class slaveries express such inherent psychological drives to dominate and enslave in industrial and post-industrial societies. Social and legal regimes of domination and suppression organize to support production imperatives with gratification of sexual desire and the reproduction of labor. Hegemonic and masochistic masculinities re-invent neo-slaveries that delineate subordinate or outlaw legal status for women and queer people. Slavery, defined as permanent legal, social or economic inability to achieve autonomous control of one's body or make independent decisions, exists as a constantly re-invented mode of dominance. Citation of gender-class cultural tradition, itself of recent origin, provides ideological reinforcement for the creation of new-old slaveries that blend elements of domination systems. Regulation of gender and sexuality, whether through religion, economic emiseration, or violence, is crucial to maintaining the massive inequalities of social power created by gender-class slaveries.

Hence the questions: will a queer slave revolt bring empowerment? Can women, abused, commodified, and trafficked as sex slaves and quasi-slaves in astonishing numbers, gain a threshold on equality and freedom through social revolt? How can gender-class commonalities join in a shared political program? What practical forms will such revolts take?

Liberal capitalism proceeds under the assumption that there can be no slave revolts because there are no slaves left, that 'slavery' is an antiquated concept or at least a hidden criminal enterprise subject to prosecution. The various Marxist traditions argue that social revolt is initiated by the disempowered under-classes, the very classes that are frequently characterized by broadly-shared antipathies towards 'queerness,' women's equality, and heterosexist absolutism. Marxist governments—viz. Cuba and Vietnam—have been as willing to foster sexual commodification and gender-class subordination, particularly via sex tourism, as liberal capitalist governments. Ironically, liberal capitalism and state Marxism have shared a false belief that they have eliminated slavery and their competing rhetoric attributed new forms of slavery to each other. Masochistic gender-class relations of domination and subordination have as much inherent potential of generating revolt as any other fundamental social inequality, irrespective of state political philosophy.

This revolt has been happening. Writing on sex and political economy in *Global Sex*, Dennis Altman argues that the last thirty years have witnessed a global queer revolution:

It is not clear that the changes in sexuality in, say, post-communist Russia or rapidly industrializing China are any greater than those wrought by the Atlantic slave trade of the eighteenth century or the massive urbanization of nineteenth century Europe. What is different however is a far denser and faster system of diffusing ideas, values and perceptions, so that a certain self-consciousness about and understanding of sexuality is arguably being universalized in a completely new way (Altman).

Where there is human revolution, there are subjects in revolt. The rapid diffusion of liberating ideas and universalizing promulgation of a new self-consciousness is the work of a queer revolt against the enslavements of sexual subordination and exploitation.

The same 'new-ness' that Altman identifies devolves into specificity of effect within particularistic cultures. Social and political queering of national cultures has become one of the ideological features of emergent globalism. This development has been strongly influenced—but far from exclusively, as right-wing nationalists and religious xenophobes assert—by the Americanization that has provided the leading definitions of globalization processes. Queer cultures and traditions are rooted in particularistic native cultures even as they draw from universalistic global culture. Political resistance to homosexual equality frequently establishes itself on rejection of homosexuality as a 'foreign' import; it distinguishes between an 'authentic' family structure and sexuality legitimated by state and divine sanction, as opposed to anathematized sexual corruption.

Queer political culture undertakes a double burden of historicizing itself within national particularisms and legitimizing emergent norms of international human rights. Implicit in the arguments of Altman and others is the problematization of relations between domestic and global queer movements and social egalitarianism, and their present and future effects in relation to politics that promote sexual and gender supremacism. This is not a critique Altman articulates, given his assertion that "I am less convinced that the term [queer] provides us with a useful political strategy or even a way of understanding power relations." Political strategies and analyses of social power will employ terminology as per their need, but we cannot agree that a queer enunciation of sexualities and power relations will have less than an overwhelming eventual impact.

Poland and eastern Europe are paradigmatic of such politics of culture clash and queer revolt, where public queer-ness constitutes a focal point of visible resistance to violent and masculinist political authority. The region has lengthy histories of political dissent that have encouraged queer-ness as a site of cultural resistance to religious dogma and conservative nationalism. Where under communism political dissidents opposed the regime, so now feminists and gay activists rebel against an oppressive gender-class system. Too, the region is undergoing a simultaneous process of incorporation into EU legal and human rights norms that will have emphatic effect towards equal citizenship. The combination of these processes potentially can provide queer resistance with explosive leverage.

The public sphere is in expanding contest, as the spread of visible gay organizing testifies. Pan-European organizing is supporting this drive towards social and political visibility. The first Christopher Street parade was organized in Russia in 1992, with the aid of Berlin gay organizations. Similarly, in Poland the current Campaign Against Homophobia and its Let Us Be Seen public advertising campaign is being assisted by the German Green Party.

Widespread violence meeting assertions of queerness and women's rights indicate the fundamental challenges that these movements embody. Senator Szyszkowska receives death threats; in Lublin, skinheads screamed at her; in Cracow, she was called a witch by the local leader of the League of Polish Families and presented with a broomstick; a Church prelate suggested that she deserved an acid attack. Mass social fears arising in the aftermath of collapse of misty visions of nation translate into violence towards palpable human symbols of difference, those who are not of the nation-that-will-not-be. After witnessing anti-gay/lesbian violence against a demonstration on the Square of the Republic in Belgrade in 2001, Jasmina Tesanović wrote:

Behind the huge, organized mass of violent, ethnically superior patriots, behind the ultra-nationalist Serb Radical Party, the homophobic organizations, the illiterate democrats, there is a bigger presence: the silent majority, including people in power, from both the former and current regime. These are the people who will say that Serbs have suffered enough disgrace and dishonor, and gays shouldn't air their shame in public, that digging up dead Albanian bodies is just about enough. These are the people who, to purify national self-esteem, would love to impose religion in schools, restrict abortion, silence the voices of ethnic or sexual minorities (Tesanović).

No less in Poland. On May 7 of this year, a queer demonstration was attacked violently in Cracow. The demonstration was part of the Festival of Gay and Lesbian Culture and it sparked a political controversy even before it began.

The city council wanted to ban it. Two Nobel Prize winners and residents of Cracow—the poets Miłosz and Szymborska—came to the defense of the gay culture festival. When the demonstration was staged, skinheads from the League of Polish Families attacked demonstrators and tried to throw caustic acid at them. Acid is what is used in eastern Europe to erase memory, minority culture, and diversity. The police defended the demonstration and the Old City of Cracow, under the hill of the royal castle, witnessed a street battle. This clash of cultures was profound and basic: an anti-woman, anti-gay, and anti-secularist right arrayed against queers and their supporters.

The slaves are revolting.

Notes

1. This is a revised version of an article that was originally published in *Bad Subjects* 69 (June 2004), available online at <http://bad.eserver.org/issues/2004/69/kitlinski_lockard.html>.

Works Cited

Altman, Dennis. *Global Sex*. Chicago: The University of Chicago Press, 2001.
Deleuze, Gilles. Présentation de Sacher-Masoch. Le froid et le cruel. Paris: Minuit, 1967. 13-115.
Krafft-Ebing, Richard von. *Psychopathia Sexualis*. New York: Bell, 1965.
Erofeyev, Viktor. "Dirty Words." *The New Yorker* September 15, 2003.
Essig, Laurie. *Queer Russia. A Story of Sex, Self, and the Other*. Durham and London: Duke University Press, 1999.
Flis, Andrzej, ed. Wyzwania wobec nauk społecznych u progu XXI wieku. Kraków: Universitas, 1998.
Freud, Sigmund. "Das ökonomische Problem des Masochismus." Vol. XIII of *Gesammelte Werke*. Frankfurt am Main: Fischer, 2001.
———. "Massenpsychologie und Ich-Analyse." Vol. XIII of *Gesammelte Werke*. Frankfurt am Main: Fischer, 2001.
———. "Triebe und Triebschicksale" Vol. X of *Gesammelte Werke*. Frankfurt am Main: Fischer, 2001.
Hegel, Georg Wilhelm. *Phänomenologie des Geistes*. Frankfurt am Main: Suhrkamp, 2001.
Kitliński, Tomek. "Z naszego sadomasochizmu." *Teksty Drugie* IBL PAN. Nr 5, 2002.
Kojève, Alexandre. Introduction à la lecture de Hegel. Leçons sur la Phenomenologie de l'Esprit professées de 1933 à 1939 à l'École des Hautes Études réunies et publieés par Raymond Queneau. Paris: Gallimard, 1979.

Kon, Igor S. "Sexuality and politics in Russia, 1700-2000." *Sexual Cultures in Europe. National Histories*. Ed. Franz X. Eder, Lesley Hall and Gert Hekma. Manchester and New York: Manchester University Press, 1999. 197-218.

Kristeva, Julia. "Un nouveau type d'intellectuel: le dissident." *Tel Quel* no. 74. Winter 1977: 3-8. ["A New Type of Intellectual: The Dissident." Trans. Sean Hand. *The Kristeva Reader*. Ed. Toril Moi. Oxford: Basil Blackwell, 1986: 292-300.]

La Boétie, Étienne de. *Discours de la servitude volontaire*. Paris: Payot, 1976.

Legutko, Ryszard. "Wymyślona partia skrzywdzonych. Identyfikacja ludzi na podstawie skłonności seksualnych jest szkodliwym absurdem." *Rzeczpospolita*. February 18, 2004.

Lockard, Joe, Tomek Kitliński, and Paweł Leszkowicz. "Monica Dreyfus." *Our Monica. Ourselves. The Clinton Affair and the National Interest*. Ed. Lauren Berlant and Lisa Duggan. New York and London: New York University Press, 2001: 203-222.

Pollock, Griselda. *Looking Back to the Future. Essays on Art, Life and Death*. Amsterdam: G+B Arts International, 2001.

Spivak, Gayatri Chakravorty. "Bonding in Difference." *The Spivak Reader*. Ed. Donna Landry and Gerald MacLean. Routledge: New York and London, 1996: 15-28.

Tesanović, Jasmina. "Why Gays Got Attacked in Belgrade. An Eyewitness Account." *The Gully. Queer Views on Everything*. June 10, 2004 <http://www.thegully.com/essays/gaymundo/010705serbia_gay_Tesanovic.html>.

Theweleit, Klaus. *Männerphantasien*. Berlin: Piper, 2000.

GOSSIP THROUGH A CRACKED DOOR: REVISITING GIRLS' BOARDING SCHOOL CULTURE[1]

DOMINIKA FERENS

When doing queer studies, we usually concern ourselves with oppositional movements and individual strategies of resistance to the heterosexual norm. Sometimes, however, we may want to look back to a time before dissent, before resistance, before the confidence that comes with feeling centered within the world of our experience. As someone who studies both racial and sexual minorities, I have long been interested in conformism, compromise and accommodation. It is those unheroic moments that have been the formative experiences of my life. By revisiting them I hope to better understand how we internalize homophobia and why we so readily assent to discrimination against ourselves and others.

This autobiographical essay is based on what I remember of my five years at a British boarding school. When I first arrived at Rosemead in 1976, at the age of twelve, it was one of a hundred or so private boarding schools in Britain. As a Polish child, I was only able to attend this school because my parents, like hundreds of other Poles, were hired by the Nigerian government to replace the British in public hospitals and at universities. When my parents stepped into the shoes of the British, albeit on very different terms, I was bundled off to boarding school according to the (post)colonial custom. Rosemead's student body was made up of the daughters of British nationals working in the Commonwealth, middle-class girls from Sussex and Surrey, and several dozen girls from Hong Kong, the West Indies, Nigeria, Iran, and Jordan (mostly daughters of government officials and urban professionals). It was a very good home away from home: the rules were tough but clear, the teachers kind, and I always looked forward to going back after the holidays. There is however, a memory I want to explore—a bugaboo that may have been the figment of my imagination but that had serious material consequences.

The Closet

Just before my graduation in 1984, a student barricaded herself in her closet-sized single room. Some time in the early spring she had stopped attending lessons; she began missing meals; she also stopped cleaning her room. An unmade bed or messy room resulted in unpleasant sanctions, even for nineteen-year-olds. Serena stacked boxes of books and clothes against the door and waded knee-deep in dirty laundry. After graduating she had intended to go on to medical school. Her father was a Hong Kong policeman. The school authorities were disoriented by such radical resistance to school rules; there was not much they could do. Had Serena been a Sussex girl they could have sent her home, but given the air fares to Hong Kong this was impractical and the end of term was only a few weeks away. During this period, I looked in on Serena only once. Poking my head through the door I saw a claustrophobic, messy cell. I said "Hi!" retreated, and never went back. Under the pressure of A-levels I refused to think about Serena, so today I have no idea how her case was eventually resolved.

I backed away from Serena's room because for some time a piece of gossip had been circulating among the older girls that Serena is a lesbian. The state of my friend's room clearly had something to do with the fact that she had been called to the headmistress's office and reprimanded for some unspecified breach of the school rules. But then I had known for years that Serena and Anita, my Caribbean friend, were girlfriends. We spent most of our study time and weekends together. Unlike the wealthier English girls, we were the daughters of doctors, teachers, and government officials who, by making sacrifices to pay our school fees, motivated us to study. Yet when through a cracked door I heard my own name included in the gossip about lesbianism at Rosemead I backed away from Serena and Anita in cold sweat.

Order

To understand this acute attack of homophobia I want to consider the heteronormative function of the girls' barding school and the institutional means of regulating the sexuality of girls aged 11-19. Traditionally, the purpose of such schools, which isolate pubescent girls from boys for most of the year, was to control their developing sexuality and, by marginalizing it, to enable them to focus on studying, on religious pursuits, playing sports, and social work. A more contemporary justification of single-sex schools and colleges for girls is the need to create a space free from male competition, in which girls might develop their intellectual abilities and leadership skills unhampered by patriarchal norms and values.

Although small schools for middle-class girls have existed in Britain since the eighteenth century, the structure of the large girls' boarding schools, dozens of which were established in the nineteenth century, was borrowed from the better-established boys' schools. In the colonial era, boys were sent to barding schools designed primarily to train the political elites and colonial administrators and to socialize them into the ideology of empire-building. I myself came to such a school from a former colony, and traveled back and forth by plane with hundreds of British children who made the journey two or three times a year. Historians have demonstrated that the power relations existing in such schools reflected the hierarchical social relations in the colonies (Sandison 1967, Gray 1913). In order to subordinate and invigilate several hundred boys at minimum cost and with maximum efficiency, the schools gave power over younger boys to those in the age group immediately above them. Sometimes the power was delegated officially; however, more often it was unofficial and therefore easily abused. Such abuses were tolerated, as they were in the colonies, where a handful of white administrators and officers governed hundreds of thousands by employing local elites. (An analogous system operates in the Polish army, where soldiers in the second year of service dominate the new recruits.)

In the twentieth century, the headmistresses of girls boarding schools, many of whom had feminist convictions, modified some of the customs and structural elements derived from boys' schools, for instance by introducing elections at various levels and reforming the curriculum which had been based on Latin and Greek. Yet the traditional structures of invigilating and disciplining students remained. How did the boarding-school girls' sexuality develop in spite of—or perhaps with the aid of—those structures? By what means was sexual discipline enforced? And how was it possible to maintain the heterosexual norm in a school where almost all contacts were homosocial?

Gossip

Krystyna Kłosińska has given these issues a good deal of thought in the Polish context, in her 1999 study *Ciało, pożądanie, ubranie* [*The Body, Desire, and Dress*]. Using Michel Foucault's revisionary analysis of theories of repressed sexuality in the Victorian era Kłosińska thus describes the world of pre-World War I boarding school girls:

> Mrs. Gierczykiewicz's establishment [described in *Przedpiekle*] is an excellent example of the game of appearances, of a type of repression that inspires. . . . In order to detect, control, and eliminate sexuality, the children's speech is subjected to invigilation. . . . watchful governesses organize a special "police" force by enlisting "Mary's children" who are immune to that reprehensible practice. Their task is eavesdropping and denouncing. Yet repression does not eliminate talk; on

the contrary, in line with the mechanism described by Foucault it incites the pupils to extraordinary discursive inventiveness. (Kłosińska 125-26)

I intend to show that despite the teachers' and supervisors' assumptions, in the walled space of the girls' boarding school, whether in Poland or in Britain, sexuality manifested itself in many guises and was regulated as much by the adults as by the girls themselves. It was simultaneously stifled and stimulated, muted and feverishly discussed, excluded and publicly performed. Foucault's understanding of power as dispersed and decentered, present at the level of human microrelations, is very useful for understanding boarding school culture. As Foucault demonstrates, it is in everyday relations within institutions such as hospitals, prisons, or schools, that bodies as disciplined subjects capable of functioning in society without supervision are produced. In this sense boarding schools are somewhat like the panopticon used in nineteenth-century prison architecture. The guard on duty in the watchtower of the panopticon sees the inside of the prisoners' cells. They, in turn, cannot see the guard and cannot know whether they are being observed at a given moment. As a pedagogical institution, the panopticon was designed to teach prisoners to always behave as if they were under observation.

The regulation of sexual behavior in a British girls' boarding schools takes place through a process of invigilation based on a hierarchy of "prefects" and "lieutenants," who are either appointed by the headmistress or elected. At Rosemead these functions were highly valued as a sign of popularity and distinction. They also gave girls a sense of responsibility and came with privileges. These were few and far between at a school where organized activities were scheduled for almost every waking hour and younger girls were allowed to go outside the school walls once a week for an hour, while seniors only once a day for an hour. The girls studied, ate, did their homework, went on walks, and even wrote letters home at prescribed time and in large groups, under the supervision of a slightly older girl. The invigilation extended to the dormitories. One bed in each large dormitory was always set aside for a girl from a higher grade.

Girls under supervision were not necessarily good, but they most definitely learned what it meant to be women. One of my first school memories, when, as a 12-year-old I lived in a dormitory with ten beds, was the following game. After "lights out," an older girl tutored us on how to tell mom and dad that we are pregnant. Although the mechanics of getting pregnant were still a mystery to some of us, each one in turn practiced this scene until we got it right. We giggled, blushed in the dark, countered or deflected our parents' potential accusations, and wondered aloud what we would do if they disowned us. Through this game we learned that being a woman is exciting and humiliating at the same time. We understood that going out with boys was desirable though it inevitably had grim consequences. The assumption that we wanted to and would eventually go out with boys went unquestioned.

During another informal lesson soon after my arrival at Rosemead I discovered the existence of the heterosexual norm. I was taught this lesson by a red-haired girl with braids, who had been told to show me around the old boarding house with labyrinthine corridors, hidden doors, stairs, and fire escapes. At the back of the building there was an disused kitchen. Striking a dramatic pose in the middle of the kitchen floor my guide said: "They once caught two girls here, stark naked, rolling around on the floor. Both of them got expelled." Horrified, I tried to imagine two bodies on the cold floor of the dark kitchen. I could not see why anyone would want to hide out there and get cold. A shiver went down my spine and I learned the lesson well.

Uniforms

Till the end of my schooldays, together with all my friends, I cultivated the heterosexual norm in spite of our sexless tweed uniform styled after boys' uniforms. After 4:00 p.m. we were allowed to change out of the uniform into "mufti." We used the evenings to compensate for the loss of "femininity." As soon as the bell rang, we ran to the dormitories wallpapered with the posters of male rock music and film stars, turned on the tape recorders full blast and listened to Rod Stewart, Sex Pistols, or Simon and Garfunkel (though Boy George was also in demand). Prancing about, we shed the regulation brown lace-up shoes, regulation brown ties with yellow and green stripes, boys' v-necked sweaters and shirts, and the hairy, bag-shaped tweed skirts that hid the detested BKs (brown knickers worn over our home underwear). We replaced these with mufti (home clothes) that exposed the shapes of our bodies: tight jeans, low-cut or see-through blouses, jewelry, and layers of makeup. Never since have I worn so many trinkets or such heavy eyeshadow. This evening uniform was also regulation.

Before St. Valentine's Day, we would send each other (and, I suspect, sometimes ourselves too) massive quantities of red and pink cards, since very few of us had boyfriends back home. The cards were anonymous or signed with the names of imaginary boys. Mail was brought to us during the morning break and handed out in a public ceremony, together with milk and biscuits. We opened our cards with great pomp and then displayed them in the dorms. Arguably, under the pretext of this heterosexual ritual at least some of the girls, consciously or not, participated in a homoerotic exchange, using it as a way to release feelings that could not be named.

Ineffectually and unsystematically the school tried to compensate for the absence of boys at Rosemead by organizing annual dances for seniors together with Lancing, a nearby boys' school of similar rank. I remember awaiting the privilege of going to a school dance more eagerly than any other. Such a dance appeared to be a great adventure since it opened the possibility of romance—it almost guaranteed romance. Somehow the privilege of going "Dancing at Lancing" passed me by; by the time I was old enough, the custom was discontinued.

At the end of the lacrosse field, over the wire fence, there was a coeducational comprehensive school. Rosemead girls were strictly forbidden to have anything to do with the comprehensive school boys. Presumably working-class boys were not suitable partners for public school girls. Our school uniform was a great impediment to meeting them. Since we had to wear it outside the school walls until the 6th form, we were very conspicuous in the town. Local homeowners knew about the ban and occasionally called in to report a sighting. The following day, during the morning assembly, the whole school was told about the unruly conduct of a uniformed girl. This system helped to maintain discipline.

Yet the local boys cared little about our school rules. If they met us in town during the day, they treated us with contempt and called us the snobs that we were; but on summer nights they would stand in groups under our windows, whispering words romantic or vulgar, and occasionally climbed the fire escapes. To put a stop to this, one year the headmistress had the window-panes facing the street painted over with white emulsion and the sash windows nailed down so we could only lower them a few inches. Perhaps the ban on meeting boys of other social classes intensified the girls' need to play out the heterosexual relation with other girls in preparation for future relations with men.

We were, however, allowed to fantasize about heterosexual love without restrictions. The teachers turned a blind eye to the unofficial circulation of teen magazines, Barbara Cartlands and Mills & Boons. They filled dormitory shelves, spilled out of chests of drawers, and were passed around under the classroom desks. The sick-bay library also stocked them, so I read quite a few when quarantined with chicken pox.

Thus, rather than disappear out of sight and hearing according to the mission of the school, knowledge about femininity and sexuality was ever-present, transmitted in whispers or under the table, from hand to hand. Knowledge about (hetero)sexuality was also dispensed in small doses in biology lessons, where we duly copied diagrams of the male and female reproductive organs from the board. Literature lessons filled in the gaps. We read *Othello*, D.H. Lawrence's *The Virgin and the Gipsy*, and Alain Fournier's *Le grand Maulnes*.

Cracking

Fantasizing was one thing, but where did adolescent girls find emotionally satisfying relations with other people when away from home for 9 months of the year, far not only from boys but also from their families? Friendship between younger and older girls (or teachers) is an old tradition in British boarding schools. The Rosemead slang for this brand of friendship was "cracking." According to Martha Vicinius, who has written about the history of homoerotic relations within the British public schools for girls, the same phenomenon has existed under many other names: crush, rave, spoon, pash, smash, gonage, and flame (Vicinius 215). The proliferation of slang words (coupled with the absence of a standard dictionary equivalent) suggests that this was a taboo relation. Such relations existed out in the open as late as the mid-nineteenth century, when friendship between girls was understood as natural training in preparation for heterosexual marriage. However, once professional sexologists appeared on the scene, defining deviations such as masturbation, sexual inversion, or lesbianism, close relations between girls and women were branded and displaced into the private, secret sphere, where they continued to blossom as late as the 1980s. Lesbianism was, in fact, so very private that when British legislators in 1929 attempted to amend the existing act penalizing homosexuality so that it would also include lesbians, Parliament rejected the proposed amendment out of concern that "women might learn something they knew nothing about" (Vicinius 228).

Vicinius interprets the rise of "cracking" in the following way: when at the end of the nineteenth century middle-class women entered universities, became professionals, and took on certain public functions, they did so with the awareness of serving as role models for younger women. "Boarding-school life during a period when women were pioneering new public roles and professional occupations especially encouraged an idealized love for an older, publicly successful woman" (Vicinius 213). It is difficult to say how many of these relations were sexually charged because they were usually described in religious discourse. They were also grounded in the ethos of self-control and self-denial. "Indeed, self-control became a key means of expressing love within the boarding-school world" (213). Nonetheless, as Vicinius rightly points out, contemporary commentators would not have condemned the phenomenon with such ferocity if they were not convinced that it had sprung out of women's sexuality. In the Victorian era, Vicinius goes on to say, "the control of one's personal feelings meant self-respect and power for Victorian women, who had for so long been considered incapable of reason. Bodily self-control became a means of knowing oneself. Self-realization subsumed the fulfillment of physical desire. Love itself was not displaced, but focused on a distant . . . inaccessible, but admired student or teacher" (215).

There was a custom at Rosemead to seek out a personal idol among the older girls, who rarely even glanced at the juniors. We would then write the words "Will you be my crack?" on decorated writing paper and discretely pass the note to our idol. If she answered "Yes," her crack would spend much of her free time writing more letters or making small gifts and expecting some form of reciprocity. This ritual, practiced throughout the school, was against the school rules, and doubly exciting because shrouded by secrecy. I do not remember ever being interested in an older girl; they scared me with their loud voices and confident manner. Occasionally, I watched them practice disco dancing through a half-open door. One of them found me in tears on the stairs and for ten minutes played piano improvisations to cheer me up. In the school's Spartan climate those were ten luxurious minutes. In later years, I myself received many "crack notes," which tickled my ego, but the younger girls' fascinations were short-lived and I no longer remember their names. I understood my role as that of older sister or emergency seamstress who sewed on buttons and mended torn hems.

Boarding school literature and countless autobiographies attest to the fact that more intense and more lasting "crushes" did exist. These had a formative influence on the younger women's subjectivity; they also profoundly affected the older girls and teachers who were the objects of adoration. Both the literary works and historical studies—and my own experience—suggest that homoeroticism frequently entered the relationships between boarding-school girls. Because it was excluded from public discourse and functioned under other names, it was largely unconscious. Named publicly and reduced to the image of two naked bodies on the kitchen floor, it became something monstrous. Even thinking about the monstrosity named lesbianism made me feel flustered and weak-kneed. Homophobia was strictly connected with the public sphere. It was, however, suspended in my friendship with Serena and Anita which sustained me through the two school years. Suspended, that is, until the nature of their relation was made public.

Coming back to Foucault's notion of power-knowledge, it is significant that the transfer of knowledge about female sexuality as well as the control of that sexuality took place almost exclusively among the girls themselves. We girls invigilated each other and maintained heterosexual discipline within the school institution. Gossip was a very useful tool for maintaining that discipline. We imposed on one another a hyper-feminine style and excluded the girls who contested this style, or were ourselves excluded. Official sanctions, such as the loss of privileges, being called into the headmistress's office, or expulsion were used very rarely. Meanwhile, unofficial sanctions, including name-calling and ostracism, were en element of everyday life. The school's mission—socializing and educating heterosexual women capable of functioning socially without supervision and prepared for marriage—was thus fulfilled.

Coda

Rosemead, as I have represented it here, is a grim place: the home of gossip, guilt, itchy tweed skirts, and nailed-down windows. Serena's friend Anita, who has kept in touch with me for over twenty years, remembers it very differently. On completing this paper I asked her for comments and have her permission to quote several fragments:

> Having come directly from a co-ed environment, it was a welcome relief to not have boys around, to feel that I could be who I wanted without all that adolescent hetero angst/energy around me. I was always aware that I was gay, so Rosemead was the perfect environment to explore this. It was so wonderful that you could be "cracked" on & that it was perfectly acceptable. I had two cracks in the third form—they are both now happily married. Serena also cracked on me, but that was just because the headmistress told us we shouldn't engage in "lesbionic" activity—her words.
>
> I spent my earlier years in Grenada dreading every school dance and activity because of the pressure to conform—which I never did. I had my first kiss in the Rosemead sickbay, lost my virginity in Main Wing, lots of 'close calls' at Winterton Lodge (Serena used to sneak into WL through my window). I could tell you many stories. I never felt under any pressure to go to a dance. Usually Helen and I would grab some food and watch TV all night. We both realized how stupid and artificial those arranged meetings were with the boy's schools. I've never read a Mills and Boon, but I think my sister had the entire collection. You may not have realized, but there were about 10 lesbians in the 6th form (well, they are now), as well as half the female teachers.
>
> What gossip about you behind the common room door? I don't think I ever heard any. I'm sure people speculated a lot about Serena and me. . . . Yes, I heard about the two lesbians in the Dorset House kitchen. Helen told me that story when I first arrived also. I was rather intrigued. . . . I don't think I would have been happy anywhere else during those years. I'm always grateful that I was sent to boarding school & that I could find my own identity away from family pressures etc. . . . I hope one day that we can actually meet up and share these stories.

The stories people tell themselves about the past have everything to do with when and why they revisit it. Anita and I could well have been talking about two different schools. Mine is full of bugaboos, hers—a lesbian paradise. Even minor details in the stories we tell suggest that we remember or invent them to keep our story coherent. "Oh, and by the way," wrote Anita, "Serena's father wasn't a policeman. He was a dentist." I wish I could hear Serena's story now.

Notes

1. I thank Izabela Kowalczyk and Edyta Zierkiewicz for provoking many Polish women to think about their childhood by organizing a conference in Poznań in 2002 titled "Looking for the little girl." I am no less indebted to Krystyna Mazur for suggesting the topic of this paper, to Aneta Dybska for finding most of the historical and sociological background sources, and to Ida Baj for a long telephone conversation which helped me to find a focus.

Works Cited

Blackmer, Corinne E. "The Finishing Touch and the Tradition of Homoerotic Girls' School Fiction." *The Review of Contemporary Fiction* 15.11 (1995): 32-39.
Foucault, Michel. *The History of Sexuality*. Vol. 1. Trans. Robert Hurley. New York: Pantheon, 1978.
Gray, Herbert Branston. *The Public Schools and the Empire*. London: Williams & Norgate, 1913.
Kłosińska Krystyna. Ciało, ubranie, pożądanie. O wczesnych powieściach Gabrieli Zapolskiej. Kraków: eFKa, 1999.
Mack, Edward. Public Schools and British Opinion Since 1860: The Relationship Between Contemporary Ideas and the Evolution of an English Institution. Westport: Greenwood Press, 1941.
Moore, Steven. "Brigid Brophy: An Introduction and Checklist." *The Review of Contemporary Fiction* 15.11 (1995): 7-11.
Sandison, Alan. *The Wheel of Empire*. London: Macmillan. 1967.
Vicinius, Martha. "Distance and Desire: Boarding School Friendships, 1870-1920." *Hidden From History: Reclaiming the Gay and Lesbian Past*. Eds. Martin Bauml Duberman, Martha Vicinius, George Chauncey, Jr. 1989. New York: New American Library Books. 212-229.

Kiss

Ruth DyckFehderau

I am so mad at Jeremy so mad I want to punch him I want to drive a tent peg through his head like the way Jael in the Bible takes a hammer and drives a tent peg through the head of the enemy king the way she waits until he's asleep and then she lines up the hammer and the peg and his temple and she bangs that hammer down and pushes that peg right through his skull and out the other side and fastens his head to the ground so his brains squirt out of his ears and eye sockets with little farting noises. With squirty little farting noises.

It all starts the afternoon after we are both baptized. Stacey's brother Jeremy and I go down to the gully beside the church. And there, in the shade of the huge old willow tree, he teaches me to smoke a pretend cigarette and he shows me his thing. It gets all swollen and purple and ugly but I look at it anyway. That is just a bad idea. Because one Sunday soon after, Jeremy waits until I'm all alone. And while no one is looking, he pushes me backwards into an empty Sunday School room, into the corner beside the blackboard, pushes his face very close to mine and whispers right in my ear, so close that I can feel his porridge breath, that I have to kiss him. I have seen his thing and so I have to kiss him. I whisper back that I have seen his thing and so I will never kiss him. He says I sound like a child but I'm baptized now so I must be an adult. And adult Christians greet each other with holy kisses, the Apostle Paul says so. Jeremy reaches with his sticky fingers and grabs the little blond hairs in my underarm and says he knows I'm an adult even though I'm just eleven. And then his stupid friends come into the room. He calls me "ba-by, ba-by" in front of them so I push him away and run from their laughing, out of the Sunday School room and around the corner and into the rehearsal room at the end of the hall and hide in the choirrobe closet where I can finally sit down and cry.

The closet smells like adult sweat and Brut and Mrs. Friesen's old lady perfume. I have to wait in there 'til my eyes don't feel red anymore. I want to drive a tent peg through Jeremy's head. I want his brains to squirt out with little farting noises. I will never let my underarm hairs show again. I wish I never got baptized. I don't want to be an adult.

Stacey is looking for me. The crack in the closet door is just big enough for me to see her running down the halls. When she can't find me anywhere out there, she comes straight to the closet. She knows I'll be there, we've been in there before. She crawls in with me and all the smelly choirrobes, and cuddles up close to me so I can feel her breath on my ear. I tell her all about what happened. Before we climb out of the closet, she whispers in my ear that we'll show him, we'll show her stupid brother Jeremy that I'm old enough to be baptized. Wednesday night, after Girls' Club for the Lord, we will kiss.

I think about this every day. I think about it the whole rest of Sunday and Monday and Tuesday and Wednesday. I think about how I have seen Stacey without clothes when we used to play baptism, just us. I know she doesn't have any ugly sausage-y purple things on her body. I think about her lips and how red they are in gym class. And I think that kissing, especially the tongue part, will taste a bit salty. Like the beeftongue my mom sometimes cooks. Like the sweat I taste when I practise kissing the inside of my arm because it's nice and soft there. I'm pretty sure Stacey's lips are soft. Really soft.

On Wednesday night, during cookies-and-juice break at Girls' Club for the Lord, Stacey and I run down to the gully beside the church where Jeremy showed me his thing. And first, well, after making sure we're alone, we giggle and hug and just touch dry lips. And then we forget to giggle, and suddenly there I am, slowly licking her lips until they are wet and the inside of her mouth even though it's already wet. And she rubs my mouth with her lips and tongue, and we both rub lips and tongues and sometimes we miss our mouths and we are just kissing and licking and licking and kissing all over our faces and necks and ears and hair and even eyes. It's a good thing we don't wear makeup yet or we'd be a *mess*. And she doesn't taste like beeftongue at all! She tastes a little bit sweet. Everything is really really good. We're late getting back to Girls' Club for the Lord. Mrs. Friesen looks at us with scolding in her face.

The next day, Thursday, I ask my mother about kissing. She says you have to be married to kiss. I ask her about the Apostle Paul's holy kisses and she says that's different, holy kisses are about God and not about Pleasure. Pleasure is just for married people. I ask her what happens to people who do Pleasure kisses and they're not married and she says they get into big trouble from their fathers and God makes them dreadfully unhappy every single day for the rest of their lives and then they go to hell. When I tell this to Stacey, she says that you need a woman *and* a man for Pleasure. We're both girls, so our kisses can't be Pleasure. They must be holy. We decide the Apostle Paul is just great and we greet each other with holy kisses all the time.

I still hate Jeremy. He told the other church boys that he showed me his thing and now they want to show me their things too. Whenever they see me and no adults are there, they pull their zippers up and down and pretend to reach in and pull it out. And they tell me to lick it until it spits or gets sticky or something. Stacey and I get mad once and yell at them to shut up and keep their stupid purple things behind their zippers or we'll drive tentpegs through their temples. They shut up for about two seconds. And then they yell "Lezbee-ans, lezbee-ans." I grab Stacey's arm and we walk away, all mature and everything, so that they will know we're really adults. When we get to an alone place, I ask her if she knows what lezbee-ans means. She says no, we can look it up in the dictionary later, we should just kiss now. We never do look up that word; kissing is just always a lot more interesting than a stupid old dictionary.

One Friday, after school, Stacey and I visit a sick cow in her barn. It's milking time, and all the cows have come in from the pasture to line up in two long rows of stalls. Stacey's dad washes all the cow udders with soap, warm water, and his puffy red hands, and latches the silver cylinders of milking machines to their teats. Those silver things just hang there, pinching and pulling at the long cow nipples. They suck and suck out all the milk. It looks very painful. Worse even than the excruciating training bras Stacey and me have to wear now that we have Developing Breasts. I go to the closest cow and whisper in her ear that she's a good person and it's not her fault she has a milking machine attached. The sick cow has no milking machine. She's in a stall at the end of the row, in the corner of the barn. She looks like every other beige cow in the barn, except that her stomach is huge and swollen and shiny, even through the hide. Stacey's dad wants to shoot her through the temple and put her into the freezer because she's too old to milk or have babies. And even though she's sick, she just keeps eating and eating like she's very hungry. Stacey's dad is worried, you can tell. He keeps saying something is very wrong with her. Something is very very wrong.

The next morning, Saturday, I go to Stacey's house early so that we can watch the vet look at the sick cow. He looks a bit funny when he sees her and pulls out a stethoscope and puts it to the cow's stomach. And starts laughing and laughing. He turns to Stacey's dad and says, she's not sick, she's Pregnant. Stacey's dad gets even more red and puffy and says that he keeps his cows under control and his bulls far away. There's no way she can be Pregnant, he says, and besides she's too old. The vet, still laughing, says that pastured cows have outsmarted farmers before, and yes, she's old, but she's definitely Pregnant and will have a calf any day now, maybe even today. He unties the cow, so that she can move around her stall, closes the stall gate, and leaves, shaking his head and laughing.

Now Stacey's dad is even more worried. He keeps saying something is very very wrong, and cows aren't the bloody Mother Mary and don't have Immaculate Conceptions. And there will be problems, big problems, at the birth because she's so old. And he will have to put on gloves that go up to his shoulder and shove his arms all the way up her bum and pull out the calf. And the new calf will be wrong, all wrong. It will have two heads, he says, two heads, and this can't be happening, this definitely can't be happening. He fills the barn with so much worry that Stacey and I feel a bit crowded and want to leave, but he stops us with his puffy hands. Stacey's family will have to take turns now, he says. Someone will have to be with the sick cow around the clock and we may as well take the first shift. If anything changes with the cow, anything at all, even her breathing, we are supposed to run and find him.

So. There we sit on bales of hay. In the corner of the barn. With nothing to do but look at a very big cow. We can't even kiss because Stacey's dad keeps coming in and out of the barn, with Jeremy right behind him, to make sure everything is fine. So we make a plan. We think, this cow is a girl and no girl wants a man to shove his arms up her bum even if he is wearing gloves up to his shoulder. And she's had babies before without any gloves or arms. We decide that if she starts having a baby on our shift, and if Stacey's dad isn't coming in here every five minutes, we will not call anyone. We will talk to her and stroke her sides and give her water to drink and hay to eat because she seems to like that a lot. We have both seen kittens be born and they didn't need any men or gloves or anything. It will all be okay. We'll bring Stacey's doctor kit, just in case. And when the baby cow is here, we decide, we will lie. We will tell Stacey's dad that we fell asleep on the watch like Peter in the Garden of Gethsemane the night before Jesus was crucified. And we will probably be punished with one of the leather straps that hang around in barns but we will bear the lashes quietly, like Jesus bore the 39 lashes the night Judas betrayed him with a holy kiss. It will be our Christian Sacrifice. And we decide that an important cow like this should have a name. At first we think Mary, but then Stacey says her dad might still be mad about the Immaculate Conception so we call her Elizabeth instead.

Well, Elizabeth doesn't do anything but eat hay and chew her cud like any ordinary beige cow for the rest of that day. It is so boring that we can hardly stay awake, and we don't use our plan at all. But the next day is Sunday. After church, while the rest of Stacey's family is in the house taking naps, we are back there again, Stacey and me, sitting on the hay bales. At first we talk about how people in stories always boil water when babies are born. We wonder if maybe we should include some hot water in our plan. And we talk about how much the milking machines must hurt cow nipples and how much we just hate excruciating training bras. Stacey pulls off her T-shirt and training bra and shows me the sore red band all the way around her ribs and under her arms. We think the milking machines must leave marks just like that. And then, without even thinking, I lean over, there in the corner of the barn, and gently lay my tongue on the raw skin at her underarm, just below the little blonde hairs, and kiss it better. Stacey turns quickly and, without even thinking, pushes her Developing Breast into my mouth. There I am. In Elizabeth's barn. Kissing and licking and licking and kissing, sucking and pulling my tongue all the way around and over Stacey's Developing Breast. And there are Stacey's hands at my temples, fastening my head right there, making sure it doesn't go anywhere else. We are very quiet and listen carefully for the barn door opening. I whisper out of the side of my mouth if this isn't sin yet, and she whispers back, shut up it's just kissing, and fills my mouth all the way up with her Developing Breast. And then I remember the cows and milking machines and I realize it can't be sin if Stacey's dad attaches sucking things to cow nipples every night. I won't even leave red marks. Even if there's no milk, and even if we have to listen very carefully for the barn door, it must just be a very holy kiss.

Then—Elizabeth makes a sound. She is more important than kissing so Stacey puts her T-shirt back on and leaves her training bra on the bales. We get up and stroke Elizabeth's sides and tell her she's a good person, but she just looks at us and rocks back and forth and chews her cud and farts a little. Sometimes she turns around and looks at us. But she doesn't do anything else. Finally, we sit back down on the boring old bales. We make ourselves comfy and we watch her very very carefully. More rocking and farting, farting and rocking. This goes on for a long time. A very long time. A very very long long time.

Suddenly we wake up to Jeremy yelling at us there in the barn. He's just standing in front of us and yelling, loud as a soldier arresting Jesus, calling us useless girls and lezbee-ans and Traitors of Gethsemane. And there, in his grubby hand, is Stacey's excruciating training bra. He runs out of the barn, calling for Stacey's dad, training bra in hand. We are in so much trouble.

And then we see her. She is the most beautiful calf you have ever seen and Elizabeth has already licked her clean. One side of her is dark brown with a white spot and the other side is white with a dark brown spot. I've never seen a cow that looks quite like her. There's a big pool of bloody mess on the stall floor but she doesn't mind at all. She's just sucking at Elizabeth's nipples like nobody's business. We jump right up, carefully because we don't want to scare the baby, and ask Elizabeth why she didn't make some noise to let us know she was having a baby. Cows make big noises, you know. Big big noises. And she just looks at us like pushing out a calf silently is something you do every Sunday afternoon.

I know the baby will grow up to be a farm cow and Stacey's dad will make her have babies when she doesn't want to and he will pull at her nipples with his red puffy hands and hook up heavy steel milking machines to her Developing Udder. And I know that Stacey and I are in more trouble than Jael's enemy king.

But you know, that's all okay. Because there she is, all alive and sucking milk and everything. And there is absolutely nothing wrong with her.

For K.

WHITER THAN SNOW

I am eleven years old. I know all about baptism. Every spring, my father fills the wheelbarrow with water and baptizes newborn puppies in it until they are dead. Well, that's what he says but I know he's joking. I'm eleven and I already know that nobody *dies* from baptism. There's baptisms in our church all the time and my father is a deacon so he cleans up after the baptisms and tells me all about them. Way back, when Stacey and I were six, we would sneak behind the pigbarn on Sunday afternoons and play baptism with Barbie dolls in the knee-deep rainwater puddle under the eavestrough. Only the Barbie dolls didn't die from baptism since they weren't alive to begin with. And they didn't have to wear any clothes because there weren't any boy dolls there. They were all, even the preacher doll, girls. Now that we are eleven and have grown too old for dolls, Stacey and I take off our clothes and play baptism and stuff, just us, since there is always plenty of water and since there are no boys around. And nobody ever dies.

My Sunday School class is studying baptism too. We're memorizing how very serious it is. Old Mr. Siemens, whose leg sometimes rubs against mine during prayer, tells us and tells us in his cracked, old voice about the Fragile Relationship between God and man. He takes us on a field trip out of our basement Sunday School room, past the teenager Sunday School rooms, past the adult Sunday School rooms, past the choir robe closet, and up the stairs to the Sanctuary. We've all been there lots of times before, but it looks very different, hollow and ancient, when the pews have no people in them. We enter from the back and walk down the centre red carpet past 36 rows of empty pews to the front where we climb the stage. Then Mr. Siemens moves the pulpit and shows us, hidden beneath the bright red carpet of the stage, sunken into the platform, the empty old falling-apart baptism tank. It's a small underground room, painted blue on the inside, and has a drain at the bottom like a bathtub. And there's a faded painting of an aimless river on the inside lid that becomes a background when the tank is open. Mr. Siemens steps down the three stairs into the tank and lies down on his back at the bottom so that we can all see the room is big enough for even the tallest man to lie comfortably at rest beneath the still waters. I ask him about the rotting wood. My father says the wood around the tank is beginning to rot because water leaks into hidden places under the pulpit and platform every time the tank is full. Mr. Siemens says he doesn't know anything about that, but Stacey whispers to me that it's probably the sin in the water and not the water itself that's making the wood rot.

After he climbs out of the tank, Mr. Siemens takes us over to the screen and overhead projector he set up in front of the stage. He shows us a transparency with a red-coloured heart on it, and a wet cloth. We look at the screen and watch Mr. Siemens wipe off the red and then we look at the cloth and see that the red is on the cloth now and not on the transparency. He says that baptism is like the cloth. It symbolizes making a man white, whiter than snow, so white that he won't even *want* to sin and dirty himself anymore. But I know it can't be the same for women, nothing in church is. My mother says girls are so dirty we could never be clean. I'm not too sure baptism works anyways. I've seen my father empty the baptism tank lots of times after other baptisms. I'm not entirely sure what sin looks like actually. But I'm pretty sure there's no sin in that water. Mr. Siemens would say that's because baptism is a *symbolic* washing. But the water is real and wet, so you'd expect to see a little bit of sin anyways. And you don't. The water is always just as clear after the baptism as it was before, though paintchips from the aimless river sometimes float in it. Except, of course, for the time the water was dirty after Peter Reimer was baptized, but he still smokes, even though he's saved, so what can you expect.

I don't really want to be baptized. No one else in my Sunday School class is getting baptized yet. But I want my father to stop noticing that I am the only one in the family who is not baptized. And besides, it will make my mother proud and will be a kind of a thank you for staying up to take care of me and make me anise-honey tea all those nights I am sick.

And so, with brand-new waterproof strawberry lipgloss, and with a snowwhite dress for afterwards to symbolize that my bright red sin is washed away, I agree to be baptized that Sunday, the hottest day of summer, along with Jeremy, who is Stacey's older brother from the teenager Sunday School class, and five other adult people. Wearing black robes with nothing but underwear underneath, we all sit in a row, thinking about serious things, looking up at the cracked wooden cross at the front of the sanctuary and at the red carpet stage (covered in plastic for today). We sit on the very front bench, just beside the throbbing organ and the sanctuary fig plant.

The baptism is very wet and very serious. The organ plays "Just As I Am Without One Plea" seven times, once for each of us. One at a time, as we are called, we walk the red plastic covered carpet to the stage, climb the three steps up the stage, and the three steps down into the tank to where the minister waits for us standing in warm water up to his waist. He asks each of us, loudly, so everyone can hear, if we've been Saved By The Blood Of The Lamb and if we Declare Jesus Christ as our Personal Saviour. And we all say, loudly, Yes I Do.

And then he says that he baptizes us In The Name Of The Father, The Son, and The Holy Ghost, and then dunks us backwards under the water. Jeremy forgets to hold his nose and makes a loud spurting noise when his head goes under. And nobody in the whole church giggles even though it is very funny. When my turn comes, I remember to hold my nose and to say all the right things. And I see, on my way out of the tank, that the plastic has a long crack in it and the red carpet underneath is just soaked.

After we have changed out of the wet black robes that cling to our bodies like drenched fur, we are given Baptism Certificates and invited outside to the Baptismal Luncheon of open-faced sandwiches and runny red Jell-O. Jeremy and I, wearing our snowwhite clothes, take our plates and Cokes down into the gully beside the church. We don't really say much while we eat. We've never really talked before and there doesn't seem to be much to say except to agree that baptism is very wet. After a while, we put the plates aside and Jeremy wonders when we will start feeling transformed. I tell him that only men feel transformed, that women really just keep on feeling wet. I keep on wishing he was Stacey. And, although I will not say this to Jeremy, I have to admit that something has died deep deep down inside me, that I wanted to feel transformed too. Despite everything my mother says about girls, I wanted to feel transformed.

Jeremy asks me if I've ever smoked. I shake my head no, and say that smoking is sin. And then I ask him to teach me. So he reaches into his vest pocket, behind his watch on a chain, and pulls out his Baptism Certificate, rips it, and rolls some grass into it. Pretending it is lit, he shows me how to hold a cigarette and how to inhale, how to suck smoke just into my mouth and then breathe half smoke and half fresh air into my lungs. We sit in silence, puffing on a soggy pretend cigarette, listening to the choir rehearsing in the background for the Afternoon Service.

> *I saw one hanging on a tree*

And then Jeremy says he'll show me something I've never seen before. He gets on his knees, unzips his pants, and, in the shade of the huge willow, pulls out his thing.

> *In agony and blood*

I am repulsed. It is unquestionably the ugliest part of a human body I have ever seen. It reminds me of uncooked sausage only more flexible. I would have thought it would be skin coloured, but in fact it is purple. And behind it is a soft-in-a-gross-way wrinkled thing hanging down. So wrinkled you would think it belonged on an old old man's body.

> *He fixed his loving eyes on me*

Jeremy begins to touch it, carefully, as if it is a sensitive object, easily hurt. It is all I can do to look at it, it is so ugly, but looking away is even harder. As he touches it, it begins to grow like a balloon being pumped full of water. Purple water. And then I realize something important. I realize why adults have pubic hair. Well, I still don't know about girls, but I'm pretty sure that boys have pubic hair to cover these goblin tumours that stick out of their smooth bodies. If I was a boy, I would grow very very long pubic hair.

As near his cross I stood.

He asks me to touch it. I tell him he is insane. I will never touch anything that looks like that, I would rather pick up soft dog doo with my fingers. He laughs and says my body is developing ahead of my brain.

Oh, can it be upon a tree my Saviour died for me?

We hear Mr. Siemens calling in the distance. The time has come for us to go inside, be congratulated, and take Holy Communion. We get up quickly and I spill a small blob of bright red jello on my dress. But that's okay, it's down at the hem where nobody will notice. As I walk towards the church, Jeremy stuffs his swollen things back into his Sunday pants, yanks up the zipper, and runs after me like a white rabbit wearing a vest.

My soul is thrilled, my heart is filled, to think he died for me.

CONTRIBUTORS

Tomasz Basiuk teaches at Warsaw University's American Studies Center. His interests include queer studies, contemporary American fiction, and theory. He was a visiting scholar at the CUNY Graduate Center in 2004-2005, and at Indiana University, Bloomington in 1991-1992. His book on William Gaddis was published in Poland in 2003. He co-edited *A Queer Mixture* (2000), the predecessor to the current volume.

Chris Bell is a PhD student at Nottingham Trent University where his work examines cultural responses to AIDS. He spends part of the year in Poland researching disability access and representation at Auschwitz and Birkenau, and teaching cultural studies classes at the Warsaw School of Social Psychology. He has published essays in *Positively Aware, The Disability Studies Reader, 2nd Edition, Culture and the Condom*, and *torquere: The Journal of the Canadian Lesbian and Gay Studies Association*. He is completing a monograph titled *Searching for Some Peace of Mind: Notes from a Black Gay HIV+ Survivor*.

Anna Borgos is a fellow of the Research Institute for Psychology, Budapest. Her research field is situated at the borderland of psychoanalysis, gender studies and literary history. She is a co-editor of periodicals *Thalassa* and *Café Bábel*, and a founding member and co-executive of Labrisz Lesbian Association. She also co-edited *Előhívott önarcképek. Leszbikus nők önéletrajzi írásai.* [Developed Self-Portraits. Lesbian Women's Autobiographical Writings] (Budapest 2003).

Anna Branach-Kallas is an assistant professor in the Department of English at Nicolaus Copernicus University, Toruń, Poland. She is the author of *In the Whirlpool of the Past: Memory, Intertextuality and History in the Fiction of Jane Urquhart* (2003) and over twenty essays on Canadian literature, which express a range of interests from corporeality, intertextuality and historiography to nationalism and postcolonialism. She is the co-editor of *Dialogues with Traditions in Canadian Literatures / Dialogues des traditions dans les littératures du Canada* (2005), *The Nation of the Other: Constructions of Nation in Contemporary Cultural and Literary Discourses* (2004) and *Exploring Canadian Identities / Vers l'exploration des identités canadiennes* (2002). She was awarded the scholarship of the Foundation for Polish Science in 2003 and 2004.

Els De Vos, Architectural Engineer and Urban Planner, is preparing a PhD at the University of Leuven on the architectural, social and gender-differentiated signification of living in 1960s-1970s Belgian Flanders. Her master's theses were "A Gender Perspective on Architecture" (2000, University of Ghent) and "Gender & Planning" (2002, University of Leuven, awarded by the Flemish Movement of Urban Planners). She presented at several conferences, including the Annual Meeting of the Society for the History of Technology (Amsterdam, 2004, Minneapolis, 2005) and the Conference of Women's History Network (Southampton, 2005). Her recent publications include: "Public Parks in Ghent's City Life. From Expression to Emancipation?" (*European Planning Studies*, 13:7, 2005).

Ruth DyckFehderau teaches in the Department of English and Film Studies at the University of Alberta, Edmonton, Canada. She has published academic and/or fiction and/or non-fiction writing in such journals and anthologies as: *Prairie Fire: A Canadian Magazine of New Writing, torquere: Journal of Canadian Lesbian and Gay Studies Association, Edmonton On Location: River City Chronicles* (ed. Zwicker), *Legacy: A Journal of American Woman Writers*.

Antke Engel is director of the Institute for Queer Theory based in Hamburg and Berlin. She received her PhD in Philosophy at Potsdam University (Germany) in 2001 and held a visiting professorship for Queer Theory at Hamburg University between 2003 and 2005. The focus of her work is on feminist and poststructuralist theory, on conceptualizations of sexuality and desire, and on the critique of representation. In her dissertation "Wider die Eindeutigkeit. Sexualität und Geschlecht im Fokus queerer Politik der Repräsentation" (Frankfurt/Main, Campus, 2002) Engel proposes a strategy of equivocation as a means of queer cultural politics. Recently she co-edited: *Queere Politik: Analysen, Kritik, Perspektiven*, issue of *femina politica. Zeitschrift für feministische Politikwissenschaft* 14 (1) 2005 and published an essay on sexuality and economy: "Das zwielichtige Verhältnis von Sexualität und Ökonomie. Repräsentationen sexueller Subjektivität im Neoliberalismus," in *Das Argument*, 2/2005: 224-236.

Dominika Ferens teaches American literature at the Department of English, Wroclaw University. Her research interests are American minority literatures and theories of race and gender. She received an MA degree from Wroclaw University, Poland, and a Ph.D. in English from the University of California,

Los Angeles. Her book *Edith and Winnifred Eaton: Chinatown Missions ad Japanese Romances*, was published by the University of Illinois Press in 2002. She is also a co-editor (with Tomasz Sikora and Tomasz Basiuk) of three volumes of essays on queer studies.

Krzysztof Fordoński studied at Adam Mickiewicz University, Poznań and University College, Galway. He received his MA in English studies in 1994 and his PhD in 2002 at the Adam Mickiewicz University. Assistant Professor at the Chair of Languages for Special Purposes, Warsaw University. His main fields of interest are English literature at the turn of the 19th and 20th century, literary translation and history of England. He has published two anthologies of English literature (1999 and 2005), monographs of William Wharton (2004) and E. M. Forster (2005), and numerous scholarly articles. He is also an active literary translator, author of translations of over thirty books, both fiction and non-fiction.

Alfons Gregori i Gomis (PhD) is Lector in Catalan at Adam Mickiewicz University, Poznań. His major research interests include identity, language and culture; ideological approaches to fantastic literature; and music and ideology. He co-edited *El Enfoque Social y Cultural en los Estudios Lingüísticos y Literarios* (2003). His recent publications include "Procesos de Formación de Identidades Colectivas en la Música Popular Contemporánea en Catalán: Los Casos de Sopa de Cabra y Els Pets" (*Iberoamericana: América Latina, España, Portugal*, 2004) and "Mecano en la Frontera Virtual: Entre el Sexo y la Muerte" (*Arte y Nuevas Tecnologías: Actas del X Congreso de la Asociación Española de Semiótica*, ed. Miguel Ángel Muro, 2004).

Tomek Kitliński did his M. Phil. under Julia Kristeva at Université Paris 7. With P. Leszkowicz, he published *Love and Democracy. Reflections on the Homosexual Question in Poland*, Kraków 2005 (in Polish with an extensive English summary). With J. Lockard and P. Leszkowicz, he authored "Monica Dreyfus" in *Our Monica, Ourselves*, L. Berlant and L. Duggan (eds.), New York University Press 2001. He contributed to *The Advocate*, *Art in America* and *thegully.com*.

Irina Kupriyanova teaches in the Psychology Department of Saratov State University, Russia, and she is a doctoral candidate in social sciences. She is also director of the Centre of Social Problems and Humanitarian Development WINGS in Saratov. She has published on various gender and queer issues in contemporary Russian society.

Joe Lockard is assistant professor of English at Arizona State University, where he teaches early American and African American literatures. His co-edited volume *Brave New Classrooms: Democratic Education and the Internet* (with Mark Pegrum) is forthcoming from Peter Lang; he has published extensively on the literature of slavery and in cultural studies.

Ewa Macura wrote her doctoral dissertation on New Women, writing and decadence. Her research interests include cultural studies, postcolonial studies, British literature and feminism. She currently teaches at the Warsaw School of Social Psychology.

Tadeusz Rachwał is Professor of English at the Warsaw School of Social Psychology. He has edited and authored books and articles on British and American culture and literature, literary theory and gender studies. His most recent publications include *Spoiling Cannibals Fun. Cannibalism and Cannibalisation in Culture and Elsewhere* (co-edited with Wojciech Kalaga: Peter Lang, 2005) and *S/He... EmbracingWrestilng Genders. Towards a Redefinition of the Political* (co-edited with Agnieszka Pantuchowicz: University of Bielsko-Biala, 2005). He is presently working on a book devoted to sobriety in the discourses of philosophy.

Tomasz Sikora teaches in the English Depratment of the University of Bielsko-Biała. He received his MA degree from Adam Mickiewicz University (1996) and a PhD in English from the University of Silesia (2001). In 2003 he published *Virtually Wild: Wilderness, Technology and the Ecology of Mediation* and over the past 4 years he has co-edited (with Dominika Ferens and Tomasz Basiuk) three volumes of essays on queer studies. His interests include gender and queer studies, as well as the discourses of nature and technology. He is a Civic Education Project Fellow.

Zuzanna Szatanik teaches at the University of Bielsko-Biała. In 2005 she defended her dissertation on feminist theory, Canadian poetry and Woman's shame, and received a PhD from the University of Silesia. Her research interests include Canadian literature, gender studies, queer studies, shame psychology and children's literature.